HEALING
Your Lost
Inner Child
Companion Workbook

HEALING
Your Lost
Inner Child
Companion Workbook

Inspired Exercises to Heal Your Codependent Relationships

ROBERT JACKMAN
MS, LCPC, NCC

 PRACTICAL WISDOM PRESS

ISBN (paperback): 978-1-7354445-2-9
ISBN (ebook): 978-1-7354445-3-6

Printed in the United States of America
The author may be reached through his website at www.theartofpracticalwisdom.com
Edited by Jessica Vineyard, Red Letter Editing, LLC, www.redletterediting.com
Book Design by Christy Collins, Constellation Book Services
Published by Practical Wisdom Press

To Drew Caldwell and All Seekers of Wisdom and Truth

CONTENTS

Introduction
 How to Use This Workbook   2
 Feelings Chart   3
 Needs Inventory   3

Part I: Exercises from *Healing Your Lost Inner Child*   9
 Exercises from Chapter 1: The Walking Wounded   11
  Your Impulsive Reactions   11
   Exercise: Your Impulsive Response Tools   11

 Exercises from Chapter 2: HEALing Emotional Wounds   15
 Functional Response Tools   15
   Exercise: Your Functional Response Tools   16
   Exercise: Functional Tools You Use Today
   (and Those You Would Like to Develop)   17
 Self-Discernment   17
   Exercise: Your Self-Discernment Skill   17

 Exercises from Chapter 4: Wounded Child, Wounded Adult   21
 How Your Impulsive Reaction Tools Developed   21
   Exercise: How Your Impulsive Tools Developed   22
 No Boundaries and/or Enmeshment   23
   Exercise: No Boundaries and/or Enmeshment   23
 Defense Mechanisms   26
 Exercise: Your Defense Mechanisms   26

 Exercises from Chapter 5: Applying the HEAL Process   27
 Creating Your Timeline   27
   Exercise: Your Timeline   27
   The Emotional Response Scale   30
   Exercise: Your Emotional Response Levels   31
 Your Childhood Household   32
   Exercise: Childhood Household Intensity Patterns   34
   Exercise: Your Treasure Chest   34
 Emotional Standouts   35
   Exercise: Your Emotional Standouts   35
 Your Age of Wounding   36
 Exercise: Determining Your Age of Wounding   36

Exercise: Simple Breathing 37

Identifying Your Triggers 37

    Exercise: Identifying Your Triggers 37

Writing Healing Letters to Yourself 39

    Letter from Your Younger Self to Your Adult Self 40

    Letter from Your Adult Self to Your Younger Self 44

    Exercise: Letter from Your Adult Self to Your Younger Self 45

Developing Functional Tools to Manage Triggering Events 46

    Exercise: Managing Triggers 46

Exercises from Chapter 6: Boundaries **48**

Internal Boundaries 48

    Exercise: Internal Boundary Commitments 49

External Boundaries 49

    Exercise: External Boundary Statements 50

Making "I" Statements 51

    Exercise: Practice "I" Statements 52

Choosing Healthy Boundaries 52

    Exercise: Practicing Healthy Boundaries 52

Bubble Boundaries 53

    Exercise: Bubble with a Window 54

    Bubble Boundary Assessment 56

Sometimes Setting Boundaries Is Hard 58

Extreme Boundaries 60

Bonus Content: Boundaries at Work and Home 62

    Boundaries in the Workplace 62

    Bonus Exercise: Boundaries at Work 63

    Boundaries with Friends and Family 68

    Bonus Exercise: Boundaries with Friends and Family 69

Three Levels of Communication 74

Picket Fence Boundaries 75

    Exercise: The Picket Fence 75

Self-Coaching 77

    Exercise: Self-Coaching 78

Exercises from Chapter 7: The Responsible Adult Self Steps Up **79**

Wounded and Functional Parts of the Self 79

    Exercise: How Your Responsible Adult Self Shows Up 80

    Exercise: Standing Up for Yourself 86

    Exercise: Strengthen Your "No" Muscle 87

    Exercise: Old Boundary Patterns 88

Developing Your New Functional Tools 90

Exercise: Who You Want to Be 91

Things You Would Like to Transform 93

    Exercise: What I Want to Transform 93

Exercises from Chapter 8: Integrating the Wounded Child **94**

Bridging the Gaps in Relationships 94

    Exercise: Creating Intentions 94

Part II: Forming a Deeper Connection with Your Inner Child **99**

Going Deeper 101

Story: The Overcompensating Inner Child 101

    Exercise: Your Impressions 103

    Exercise: A Quick Snapshot 103

Daily Connection with Your Inner Child 104

    Exercise: Connect with Your Inner Child 104

    Exercise: Give Your Inner Child a Voice 104

A Deeper Connection with Your Lost Inner Child 107

    Exercise: Your Wounded Child Perspective 107

Emotional Response Tools 113

Wounded Emotional Response Tools 113

    Exercise: Your Wounded Emotional Response Tools 113

Functional Emotional Response Tools 116

    Exercise: Your Functional Emotional Response Tools 116

Triggers 119

What Triggers You 119

    Exercise: What Triggers You 119

    Exercise: Gentle Detachment from Triggers 120

    Exercise: Your Personal Theme 122

Healing Letters Redux 123

Healing Letters Mad Libs˜ Style 123

    Exercise: Healing Letters Mad Libs Style 123

Healing Letters Review 126

Codependency 127

Codependency and Relationships 127

Judging Codependent Behaviors 128

Codependency as an Adult 128

    Story: The Child Who Thought He Wasn't Worth Loving 129

    Exercise: Codependent Behaviors Assessment 131

Circle of Connection 134

Your Circle of Connection 134

    Exercise: Your Circle of Connection 134

    Exercise: Friends and Family Circle Review 136

Exercise: How You Change Yourself for Others 139

Exercise: Toxic People in Your Life 141

Hurt People Find Hurt People 145

Your Wounded Mirror 145

Exercise: Your Wounded Mirror 145

Wounded Partnerships 148

I Don't Want to Talk about It 149

Grieving the Loss of the Familiar 151

Grieving and Boundary Statements 152

Relationship Transformations 153

Transforming Your Relationships 154

Exercise: Transforming Your Relationships 155

Creating Deeper, Safer Connections 156

Your Safe Connections 156

Exercise: Making Deeper Connections 156

Creating a More Positive Outlook 159

Negative Self-Talk 159

Exercise: A More Positive Outlook 159

Expanding and Contracting 162

Exercise: Feeling Contracted and Feeling Expanded 162

Storytelling: Fact or Fiction 165

Making Up Stories 165

Exercise: Are You a Storyteller? 167

Shame 169

The Shadow of Shame Monster 169

Exercise: The Shadow of Shame Exposed 170

Speaking Your Truth 173

Using "I" Statements 173

Exercise: Using "I" Statements to Express Your Truth 174

Symbolic Letter Writing 178

Symbolic Letters 178

Exercise: Symbolic Letter Writing 178

Filtering 181

Your Personal Filter 181

Exercise: What Is Clogging Your Filter? 182

Feeling Stronger Every Day 184

A New Part of You 184

Exercise: Rename the Healing Part 184

Letting Go of Attachment to an Outcome 187

Exercise: Observing Your Expectations 188

Self-Nurturing 191

Elements of Self-Care 191

Exercise: Practice Nurturing Narratives 192

INTRODUCTION

In the book *Healing Your Lost Inner Child*, you learned that inner child work is a reconnection with the unhealed part of you that keeps showing up and playing out the same dramas until it is acknowledged and healed. This rejoining is an opportunity for you to go within and form a heartfelt connection with the lost inner child, which holds a great treasure: your unhealed emotional pain. When you give this part a voice, it softens and reveals your core wounding, illustrating how you got to this place. The lost inner child is deep inside, waiting patiently to give you answers that will help you better understand yourself and your wisdom.

To become a conscious creator in your life you need to heal and move away from the impulsive reactivity of the lost inner child. The HEAL process—Healing and Embracing an Authentic Life —is a road map on your journey of discovery toward healing this part of you.

This companion workbook will help you to continue the hard work you did while working through the book. The exercises in this workbook will help you to develop an even deeper healing connection with your lost inner child. All of the exercises and examples are based on the core concepts described in the book, and while you can use this workbook independently from reading the book, you will receive a deeper level of healing if you know the core concepts and have gone through the HEAL process.

This workbook is designed to help you create a deeper understanding of the character and voice of your inner child so that you can clearly understand when, where, and how your wounded part shows up. These are your wounded emotional response tools, such as avoiding, lying, ignoring, and being passive-aggressive. Once you understand when and how that wounded codependent part presents itself in your day-to-day life, you will be able to make clearer decisions based on this greater understanding.

How to Use This Workbook

Part I has the same exercises in the same order as each chapter in the book. If you have purchased the workbook along with the book, you can do all of the exercises here instead of using a separate notebook. If you have already completed the book and exercises separately, you may consider doing them a second time in the workbook to see if you answer the questions in the same way today as you did when you started your healing journey.

Part II has all new material not found in the book, and will help you to go to a deeper level within by expanding on the knowledge and insights you gained from the book. Some of the exercises in Part II are variations of the exercises, lists, and letters you completed in the book. There are more examples of inner child work, codependency, and boundary setting in relationships and at work. You will also learn to develop a self-nurturing plan. As you explore Part II, you will find a lot of new material to help you understand your inner child more comprehensively.

As you go through the workbook, use intentional thought as you complete the exercises, but don't overthink your answers. Often your first instinct is how you really feel.

The fill-in-the-blank exercises are meant to help you gain insights into how you think and feel about a certain subject at that moment in time. These exercises will not give you answers for what to do for these issues, but rather, they will help you to develop a deeper introspection of yourself. As you go through the workbook, you may find that you start to remember more from your past that you may want to explore. You now have the tools to do so, and you can include your new insights and thoughts into the steps of the HEAL process to help you gain insights and healing.

Much of therapy work is about teaching introspection, and the exercises in Part II are designed to help you answer on your own the questions that a therapist may ask in a psychotherapy session. You can choose which exercises speak to you at the given moment. The exercises are about creating an understanding within yourself, and to learn to love, respect, and honor yourself as you were authentically aligned at birth.

It is not easy to do this work, but once you have worked through your issues, you will surely feel better. Living life, being in relationships, and doing your life's work becomes easier. This sense of emotional freedom takes focused effort and a level of commitment. You are continuing on a great journey of self-discovery. Enjoy the journey, and remember to be gentle with yourself throughout the process. Get ready for some *aha* moments!

**We have to get out of our heads and
into our hearts to heal and remember.**

Feelings Chart

Being able to identify a word that most fittingly describes how you feel in the moment is a great gift. When you use the best word you can think of to describe a feeling you are experiencing, you can relax in the recognition that you are linking up your feelings with your conscious expression. You are attuning yourself to your true nature, using your words to find agency within, and recognizing that, yes, this is how you are feeling right now.

As you are doing this work, refer to the Feelings Chart in table 1, created by the Center for Nonviolent Communication.[1] Notice that feeling words are put into two categories: when your needs are satisfied and when they are not met. The words represent feelings of emotional states and physical sensations that you want to express. This list is meant as a guide. As you progress, you may have some words of your own that you would like to add to the chart.

Needs Inventory

Needs are an essential part of our lives. Our needs are things that are necessary for us to live and as you will see, they represent much more than just food, clothing and shelter. Needs are not luxuries, they are what fulfill our sense of self worth and esteem at a deep fundamental level. Identifying your needs will help you understand yourself better and you will be able to communicate more clearly your needs to others. Needs will take you into a deeper connection with yourself and they are different from wants. Wants are things or aspects that are fleeting or things of desire that do not have lasting value.

Look over the list in table 2, see what needs are being met in your life right now and identify the needs you want to manifest.[2]

---

1   (c) 2005 by Center for Nonviolent Communication. Website: www.cnvc.org; email: cnvc@cnvc.org; phone: +1.505.244.4041.

2   (c) 2005 by Center for Nonviolent Communication. Website: www.cnvc.org; email: cnvc@cnvc.org; phone: +1.505.244.4041.

Table 1: Feelings when your needs are satisfied

AFFECTIONATE
compassionate
friendly
loving
open hearted
sympathetic
tender
warm

ENGAGED
absorbed
alert
curious
engrossed
enchanted
entranced
fascinated
interested
intrigued
involved
spellbound
stimulated

HOPEFUL
expectant
encouraged
optimistic

CONFIDENT
empowered
open
proud
safe
secure

EXCITED
amazed
animated
ardent
aroused
astonished
dazzled
eager
energetic
enthusiastic
giddy
invigorated
lively
passionate
surprised
vibrant

GRATEFUL
appreciative
moved
thankful
touched

INSPIRED
amazed
awed
wonder

JOYFUL
amused
delighted
glad
happy
jubilant
pleased
tickled

EXHILARATED
blissful
ecstatic
elated
enthralled
exuberant
radiant
rapturous
thrilled

PEACEFUL
calm
clear headed
comfortable
centered
content
equanimous
fulfilled
mellow
quiet
relaxed
relieved
satisfied
serene
still
tranquil
trusting

REFRESHED
enlivened
rejuvenated
renewed
rested
restored
revived

Feelings when your needs are not satisfied

AFRAID
apprehensive
dread
foreboding
frightened
mistrustful
panicked
petrified
scared
suspicious
terrified
wary
worried

ANNOYED
aggravated
dismayed
disgruntled
displeased
exasperated
frustrated
impatient
irritated
irked

ANGRY
enraged
furious
incensed
indignant
irate
livid
outraged
resentful

AVERSION
animosity
appalled
contempt
disgusted
dislike
hate
horrified
hostile
repulsed

CONFUSED
ambivalent
baffled
bewildered
dazed
hesitant
lost
mystified
perplexed
puzzled
torn

DISCONNECTED
alienated
aloof
apathetic
bored
cold
detached
distant
distracted
indifferent
numb
removed
uninterested
withdrawn

DISQUIET
agitated
alarmed
discombobulated
disconcerted
disturbed
perturbed
rattled
restless
shocked
startled
surprised
troubled
turbulent
turmoil
uncomfortable
uneasy
unnerved
unsettled
upset

EMBARRASSED
ashamed
chagrined
flustered
guilty
mortified
self-conscious

FATIGUE
beat
burnt out
depleted
exhausted
lethargic
listless
sleepy
tired
weary
worn out

PAIN
agony
anguished
bereaved
devastated
grief
heartbroken
hurt
lonely
miserable
regretful
remorseful

Feelings when your needs are not satisfied, cont.

SAD	TENSE	VULNERABLE	YEARNING
depressed	anxious	fragile	envious
dejected	cranky	guarded	jealous
despair	distressed	helpless	longing
despondent	distraught	insecure	nostalgic
disappointed	edgy	leery	pining
discouraged	fidgety	reserved	wistful
disheartened	frazzled	sensitive	
forlorn	irritable	shaky	
gloomy	jittery		
heavy hearted	nervous		
hopeless	overwhelmed		
melancholy	restless		
unhappy	stressed out		
wretched			

Table 2: Needs Inventory

CONNECTION	CONNECTION	HONESTY	MEANING
acceptance	*continued*	authenticity	awareness
affection	safety	integrity	celebration of life
appreciation	security	presence	challenge
belonging	stability		clarity
cooperation	support	PLAY	competence
communication	to know and	joy	consciousness
closeness	be known	humor	contribution
community	to see and be seen		creativity
companionship	to understand and	PEACE	discovery
compassion	be understood	beauty	efficacy
consideration	trust	communion	effectiveness
consistency	warmth	ease	growth
empathy		equality	hope
inclusion	PHYSICAL	harmony	learning
intimacy	WELL-BEING	inspiration	mourning
love	air	order	participation
mutuality	food		purpose
nurturing	movement/exercise	AUTONOMY	self-expression
respect/self-respect	rest/sleep	choice	stimulation
	sexual expression	freedom	to matter
	safety	independence	understanding
	shelter	space	
	touch	spontaneity	
	water		

PART I

Exercises from *Healing Your Lost Inner Child*

Love has come to rule and transform.
Stay awake, my heart, stay awake.
—Rumi

EXERCISES FROM CHAPTER 1

THE WALKING WOUNDED

As you learned in the book, your impulsive reactions were learned at a young age to help you cope with a level of chaos or dysfunction within your childhood family. These codependent reactions were your best attempt to find a way to make your world feel as functional, safe, and controlled as you could. Your wise inner child has carried these reactions for all of these years, and now you can begin to acknowledge and heal those reactions so you don't have to keep repeating these patterns.

Your Impulsive Reactions

Do you know what your impulsive reactions are? In this exercise you will explore some of the wounded emotional response tools you use as an adult but were crafted in childhood.

The following is a list of common impulsive reactions developed in childhood and then carried into adulthood. They are the reactions that bring our wounding to the foreground when triggered. As you read through the list, think of the reactions you learned as a child or those you have used in your adult life. Just gently observe, and avoid condemning or harshly judging yourself.

EXERCISE: YOUR IMPULSIVE RESPONSE TOOLS

Highlight the tools you learned as a child, and circle the ones you still use as an adult. (Mark this exercise, as you will be coming back to it often throughout the workbook.)

- Shutting down or withdrawing emotionally
C • Being super quiet so as not to be noticed *peacemaker*
A • Acting passive-aggressive so as not to show your anger
- Blaming

perfectionism & control is the opposite of chaos but it is a demanding master

- Getting too involved in a relationship too quickly
- Oversharing intimate details about yourself too quickly
- Lying
- Feeling as if you have no needs (needless)
- Feeling as if you have no desires or dreams (wantless)
- Self-harming as a way to self-soothe
- Sabotaging
- Overspending money you don't have to fill up a hole inside
- Projecting or mind-reading what others think or feel about you
- Using drugs, alcohol, food, pills, weed, or other substances to escape or cope
- Pushing emotions down until they manifest as anxiety or depression
- Seeking attention
- Sneaking around
- Hiding (literally)
- Overworking
- Overcompensating
- Bullying others
- Checking out
- Playing the victim for attention
- Feeling less-than
- Feeling greater-than
- Making yourself smaller so you can feel bigger
- Getting bigger so others feel smaller
- Attacking others out of anger because of the shame you feel
- Overcompensating (pretending to have it all together but feeling like an imposter)
- Rebelling at authority or those who you think are trying to control you
- Yelling
- Feeling responsible for everything bad that happens
- Getting lost in self-loathing
- Avoiding conflict
- Saying "I'm sorry" a lot
- Giving your power away
- Making everyone else more important
- Enabling others' destructive habits and avoiding real discussions
- Trying to be a peacemaker

- Acting as a caretaker
- Being a fixer
- Getting really loud or demonstrative so others hear and see you
- Ignoring others so they don't hurt you
- Giving too much or too little
- Ignoring your gut reaction or intuition
- Doubting yourself
- Being impulsive
- Being irrational
- Being moody
- Brooding
- Throwing temper tantrums
- Being clingy
- Pushing away
- Whining
- Being sarcastic
- Escaping through pornography or masturbation
- Using sex, shopping, and other activities to avoid your feelings
- Wanting to escape
- Saying you just wish you were dead (but not wanting to die)
- Wanting to be out of pain (not necessarily by dying)
- Being greedy
- Gambling
- Feeling anxious
- Changing yourself for someone else's comfort
- Being overly controlling
- Manipulating others
- Being obsessive
- Being petty

These are just some of the wounded emotional response tools you may have developed as coping skills while dealing with chaotic, uncertain, and disrupted households when you were young. They are the impulsive reactions you may use when you later sit back and say to yourself, *Why did I do that?*

(If you feel overwhelmed by reading over the list in this exercise, take a deep breath. As you go through this process you will gain clarity as to why you do these things, and learn ways to heal this wounding.)

Look within to see what other wounded tools you use that aren't listed here. Make a note of what you find, as this insight will give you clues to help you on your healing journey. You may also want to look back over your list and begin to connect with how, when, where, and why you developed these wounded emotional responses. The impulsive reactions you identify now will show up throughout your work within the HEAL process.)

HEALING EMOTIONAL WOUNDS

Your functional response tools are the reactions you have to situations when you have clarity and are sure of yourself. You know at a deep level that they are your best response for the situation, and you are not reacting from an out-of-control emotional place but from grounded authenticity. Your functional response tools represent the best part of you that shows up in a situation.

Functional Response Tools

Your functional response tools developed over time, just like your wounded tools did. These thoughts, feelings, and behaviors helped you when you were a child and may still be helping you today. They are the attributes and responses that help you stay grounded and connected to your authentic self.

The following list provides examples of functional response tools:

- Feeling proud of yourself even when you aren't acknowledged by someone else
- Recognizing the healthy and positive actions and choices you need to help you through your day
- Acknowledging the friends who are good for you and encourage you
- Honoring yourself when you have accomplished something that was really challenging to do
- Respecting yourself and your decisions

- Recognizing when relationships are reciprocal and when they are not
- Knowing that you make the best choices possible each day, even if they are not perfect
- Encouraging yourself to move forward and finding the motivation to do things that you know are right for you
- Loving those parts of yourself that still need care so they will heal
- Asking for help from others
- Practicing good self-care by getting extra rest when you need to, or participating in hobbies or sports as a way to relax
- Being emotionally vulnerable with others whom you trust
- Connecting with family and friends who help you feel whole
- Discerning who or what is working for you and who or what is working against you

Once you have a healed perspective, your functional tools will stand out to you because you will see the positive, healthy results you get from using them. It will then become easier to access these tools instead of wounded tools.

EXERCISE: YOUR FUNCTIONAL RESPONSE TOOLS

Using the previous list of functional response tools, think about some of the tools that help you today. Write down the ones you use and the ones you would like to develop. Which tools do you intuitively know you need to develop?

_____

_____

Think about the functional response tools that others in your life use that you don't. Which ones would you like to start using? Write them down, too.

_____

_____

EXERCISE: FUNCTIONAL TOOLS YOU USE TODAY
(AND THOSE YOU WOULD LIKE TO DEVELOP)

When do you feel most proud of yourself? When do you feel that the best of you showed up for yourself or someone else? How do you show yourself and others that you care for them, sometimes without saying a word? These are your functional tools and how you bring your responsible adult self into your present-day life. Write down what you want to do more of to show yourself and others that you embody love, care and respect.

_____

_____

Self-Discernment

Discernment is our ability to look within ourselves and to know what is best for us at any given moment. It is a learned skill that is aligned with our authentic self for us to know if something is right or not. We learn the art of discernment by trusting ourselves and our gut reaction to situations. The more we have a clear and open channel to ourselves, the more accurate our discernment is.

EXERCISE: YOUR SELF-DISCERNMENT SKILL

Take a few moments to determine your skill at self-discernment by answering the following questions. If you need more prompts, you can refer to the self-reflection questions in the introduction. Answer the following questions that apply to you:

What is jamming your authentic, clear perception of self?

_____

_____

How do you sabotage your life?

_____

_____

What negative beliefs do you have about yourself? Where did they come from?

_____

_____

Why is it hard some days to know you are loved?

_____

_____

What sort of situation or person feels good to you? Why?

_____

_____

What sort of situation or person does not feel good to you? Why?

_____

_____

Why do you let others influence your choices most of the time?

_____

_____

Whose voice is inside your head?

_____

_____

Why do you think you doubt a choice or decision you made, and then backtrack?

_____

_____

How often do you make choices without even thinking about them?

_____

_____

In what situations are you mindful of your choices? Why these situations and not others?

_____

_____

With whom in your life do you have a difficult time knowing where they end and you begin?

_____

_____

What feeling or idea do you carry that you adopted from someone else?

_____

_____

From whom, where, or how did you acquire the belief that you are less-than?

_____

_____

Look over your answers. What themes do you see? Are there situations or names that you listed more than twice? What is the message you are discovering about your level of discernment?

If you were able to answer these questions easily, you may have a strong connection with yourself, know yourself very well, and make good choices. If you filled a page or two with responses, and wrote down many of the same people and situations, then you may need to work on gaining clarity by using your discernment. If you have a lot of drama and dysfunction in your life, you probably need to do more work in your ability to discern situations and other people.

You have the ability to be discerning; you simply learned to give away your power to others so they would like or love you. You made their needs more important than your own because of poor boundary setting.

Discernment is about clarity within ourselves, not confusion. If you are confused about why, when, and how you think or feel about something, then keep reading. Each step of the HEAL process will help you to develop a clear idea and connection to who you really are.

WOUNDED CHILD, WOUNDED ADULT

Remember that growing up, your responses to any given situation were based on all of the knowledge you had of yourself as a child and of your family. At the time, you developed your responses to fit your family or relationship-specific circumstances. This skill set is highly specialized to a time and place, but chances are you have carried these impulsive reactions into your adult life.

How Your Impulsive Reaction Tools Developed

The following exercise is a continuation of "Exercise: Your Impulsive Response Tools" in chapter 1. Before you start this exercise, please review your answers to that exercise to refresh your mind.

To give you an example of how to work through the following exercise, let's use the impulsive response tool of *I yell at others when I feel out of control.* If this is one of your impulsive tools, ask yourself why you needed that tool in your early life. For example, *I needed this tool to fight back when I felt defenseless.* Think about what, where, why, and for whom you created this impulsive response tool. Think about the times you felt helpless, uncertain, scared, and worried. For example, *I created this tool as my defense when my older brother would beat me up.* Write down your answers next to each impulsive tool.

You can also write down who you learned the tool from, if this applies. Was it in response to something going on in your life, or to what someone said or did to you? Did you see someone else doing it, or was it something that was put on you? A common thought during this exercise is, *I don't know why. I have just always done it this way.* That is fine. Write this down, too. We are so familiar with ourselves that even our dysfunctional actions and reactions feel normal.

EXERCISE: HOW YOUR IMPULSIVE TOOLS DEVELOPED

Write; How, Why and When your impulsive tools developed:

_____

_____

_____

_____

Once you have your answers, carefully look them over as a whole. Do you see any repeating patterns? Write them down. For example, you may discover the pattern of choosing partners who you give power to or who behave as though they have power over you. Once you have identified a pattern, think about how it applies to your past and current relationships. Do you think you choose friends or partners based on this pattern? How is this related to your impulsive response tools?

_____

_____

This exercise is to help you begin to understand that you learned your emotionally wounded responses for a reason. You weren't born with these wounded tools; you created and developed them to help you cope. As you move through the HEAL process, you will discern whether or not these tools still serve you and whether or not you want to keep using them.

In the space below, write out the wounded impulsive response tools you use most often as an adult (the ones you circled in the chapter 1 exercise), why you use them, and if they still serve you:

_____

_____

_____

_____

No Boundaries and/or Enmeshment

Do you think you have little or no boundaries with others? Do you think you might be enmeshed with family members or friends as a result? Having no boundaries means that you aren't paying any attention to what is OK and not OK for you to do, think, or have others do to you. Enmeshment is having flexible and fuzzy boundaries with yourself and others, when you are in everyone else's business. It can be difficult to look inward at this part of yourself, but looking at your ability to set or not set boundaries is an important step toward creating a sense of safety for the wounded part inside.

EXERCISE: NO BOUNDARIES AND/OR ENMESHMENT

Carefully consider the following questions, and write out your answers to the ones that have meaning for you. As you do so, just observe, don't condemn yourself. There is no right or wrong; you are just exploring where you are right now with your boundaries. As you read over the list, mark next to each if there is a person or situation that stands out for you when you read the question. You will use these answers when you learn to set healthy boundaries later in the workbook.

Do I let others walk all over me?

_____

Do I play the victim? If so, why do I give others power over me?

_____

Do I want to run away because I am exhausted from trying to do everything for everyone?

_____

Do I wish that others could read my mind and just know what I need?

_____

Do I think, *If they loved me, they would know what I need*?

_____

Do I test others to see how much they love me?

_____

Do I try to control others indirectly?

_____

Do I hope that others will pick up on clues when I feel angry, sad, or frustrated?

_____

Do I want to be invisible but seen at the same time?

_____

Do I let others dictate how I feel or how I should feel about myself?

_____

Do I think others are talking about me behind my back?

_____

Do I need to know what everyone else is doing?

_____

Do I give others my opinion even if they don't want it?

_____

Do I let others determine my reality because I don't know what I want?

_____

Do I feel unworthy to set boundaries or say no to others?

_____

Do I feel that I don't deserve anything?

_____

Do I try to help others with their lives because mine is a mess?

_____

Do I avoid taking ownership for anything?

_____

Do I disrespect what others think or believe?

_____

Do I doubt and question everyone?

_____

Do I doubt and question myself?

_____

Look over the questions you answered yes to. Do you see any trends, or are there people and situations that keep showing up? These thoughts and behaviors are how your lack of boundaries or enmeshment show up in your relationships. They are a reflection of the healing work that is needed; they are not good or bad, they just are.

Defense Mechanisms

Many people don't want to look at their childhood woundings because doing so is painful. If you have this reaction, you may be compartmentalizing these painful experiences and pretending that things weren't that bad. *I turned out OK, didn't I?* Such rationalizations give you an excuse to avoid feeling or looking at things. However, as you have learned in the book, touching on the events you have experienced is not going to kill you. It may hurt or sting, but you are stronger than you know, and with some self-care you will get through this process intact and feel much better.

EXERCISE: YOUR DEFENSE MECHANISMS

Ask yourself how, when, why, and with whom you may be doing one of the following in your life:

- Discounting – Set aside the temptation to discount or minimize the difficult or traumatic experiences you had growing up. In other words, don't normalize your emotional pain. ("It wasn't that bad.")
- Normalizing the abnormal – Resist the urge to make the abnormal normal. ("Everyone was beaten.")
- Protecting others – Resist the urge to protect your parents, guardians, family members, and others. This work is not about dishonoring them, it is about honoring yourself.
- Denying that healing is possible – Avoid the temptation to think you can't heal because you can't change the past. ("Why would I want to go back and look at that if I can't change it? What has happened, happened, and nothing can be done.")
- Avoiding bad memories – Let go of the idea that you can heal without exploring bad memories. It takes courage to heal, and you are worth it. ("I can't remember much of what happened, and what I do remember I don't like, so why go there?")

EXERCISES FROM CHAPTER 5
APPLYING THE HEAL PROCESS

You carry within you an incredible history of emotional memories and a timeline of significant events that shaped your sense of self and how you look at the world. Creating your timeline is one of the more significant steps of the HEAL process because the work you put into identifying these key aspects of your early life will create a roadmap for healing your life today.

Creating Your Timeline

It is time to take a deep dive into your own timeline and identify your emotional standouts. Take your time with this process, and be gentle with yourself. Set aside plenty of time, and be in a place where you won't be disturbed or interrupted. You are about to do some deeply personal and important work. All of that said, do not overthink it. This is your story, and you know the details.

Read the next several paragraphs to see how to recall standout events. Next to the timeline in Figure 1, on the next page, make marks to denote the years between birth and age twenty. Next to each year, you will write down a standout event from that age that you can recall easily.

EXERCISE: YOUR TIMELINE

Be quiet and let your mind wander. Begin to picture the events of your past unfolding like a movie. As your mind flows, jot down some events that stand out. Write down short phrases along the timeline next to the age you were when each event occurred. Some people write out incredibly detailed memories, and others write brief notes. Do what works for you.

Avoid discounting events by thinking they weren't a big deal or that those things happened to everyone. That may be true, but it will all contribute to your understanding of yourself. Just let things come up. Continue writing these events on your timeline.

Some situations may be uncomfortable to think about, so for now just make a mark or write down just enough of a description to remind you later. Suppose you remember an event from when you were seven when someone touched you inappropriately and it felt icky. Just write down "icky." This work is not about resurfacing trauma just to get through the exercise, so be gentle with yourself as you go through this process.

Continue filling out your timeline. You may find that you have more information to write down as you get into your teenage years, which is normal.

FIGURE 1. TIMELINE, BIRTH TO AGE TWENTY

If you have difficulty remembering events, it may help to talk with a trusted friend or relative who knew you before you were twenty. If you feel comfortable, tell them what you are doing and see if they have any insights into your early life. They might remember something about you that stands out for them but for you it was just another day. If you can't remember anything, especially from a young age, don't put anything for that age. Your emotional standouts will help you determine your age of wounding.

The Emotional Response Scale

Once you have filled in your timeline, you are ready to use the Emotional Response Scale to determine the level of intensity that each event holds for you. This exercise will help you to better define how you feel about these events today. It is based on your subjective measurement, so honoring how you feel about each event is important. These ratings are going to help you determine your age of wounding.

The Emotional Response Scale uses a scale of 0 through 10, with 0 having the lowest emotional intensity (neutral, happy, or joyful) and 10 the highest emotional intensity (great shame or sadness). The scale is not used to rate an event as "good" or "bad." It simply rates the level of intensity inside of you when you recall the event.

You will be using the following descriptions of the Emotional Response Scale to determine the level of intensity of each standout event on your timeline. Mark each emotional standout on your timeline with a rating from the scale.

LOW INTENSITY (0 – 3)

Examples of a low intensity rating are:

- This event really bothered me as a kid, but the memory doesn't bother me now.
- I feel neutral most of the time when I remember this event.
- This event was happy and full of joy.
- I just shrug over this memory, and I can move on.
- I can be around the person who hurt me, I have forgiven them and let it go, and it is not a big deal anymore.
- I used to get really angry at this situation or person, but I have worked through the pain and have a greater perspective today.

MID-RANGE INTENSITY (4 – 6)

Examples of a mid-range intensity rating are:

- I have seen pictures of a time when I know things weren't good, but I look happy, so I am confused about how I should feel.
- Sometimes I am upset about what happened to me but not all the time.
- I can be around these people or situations sometimes but not all the time.
- This type of situation (family dynamic or chronic issue) still creates turmoil in my life; I don't like it and want it to go away.
- When I remember this event it stings, but the bad or shameful feeling comes and goes.

HIGH INTENSITY (7 – 10)

- I get really angry or feel hurt or sad whenever I think of what happened.
- I withdraw, get very quiet, and shut down whenever I think of what happened.
- I have a physical reaction if I am in a certain area or around people who remind me of my abuser.
- I am filled with shame and pain when I remember this event.
- I wish this memory would just go away. I want to erase the whole event.
- I dissociate or "zone out" when I think of this event or when I get triggered. (This is a level 10 intensity.)

EXERCISE: YOUR EMOTIONAL RESPONSE LEVELS

Look over your timeline, and as you remember each situation, rate the intensity of the feeling between 0 and 10. Write this number down next to each event using a colored pen or pencil. This information is just for you, so be honest with yourself.

Once you have rated each event, sit back and look over your timeline again. What does this big picture tell you about your early life? Are there a lot of low- to mid-range ratings next to each event? Or did you rate many of them mid- to high-intensity? What do the ratings reveal? Are the high-intensity ratings clumped together, or are they scattered throughout the timeline?

Remember that the ratings exercise is a way to measure the events of your life and to recognize that some situations were very intense. It can help you to determine an age of wounding that will help you to see the symptoms manifesting in your adult life.

Your Childhood Household

Another way to look at your timeline and the events that happened in your first two decades is to think of your childhood household and all of its members, and what the interactions were like. The following are descriptions of how a household may have felt as it relates to the Emotional Response Scale, and how growing up in such a household may manifest emotionally and relationally in your adult life.

LOW-INTENSITY HOUSEHOLD

If you grew up in a household with an overall low-intensity rating, you probably felt good about yourself most of the time. There were situations that occurred now and then that upset you, but nothing bizarre or odd. You were able to brush off most things that were unpleasant. You met and kept friends, and even though life wasn't perfect, you had more happy times than angry or hurtful times. Consistent, loving adults were always present. The adults had their own issues, but they could regulate their emotions and provide a flow of stable love and reflection back to you. You felt validated, honored, and cherished by the adults in your life. You still feel this feeling as a warm glow in your heart or belly when you think of specific times growing up.

How a low-intensity household experience may manifest in adult life

As an adult, you are able to check in with your partner or friends when things are bothering you. The overall good feeling from your childhood experiences carried over into your adult experiences. Your adulthood mirrors the type of childhood and family environment that you had growing up.

MID-RANGE INTENSITY HOUSEHOLD

If you grew up in a household with an overall mid-range intensity rating, you probably feel that your home life was OK for the most part, but you didn't always feel OK. What was happening on the outside didn't always match the inside, like the beautiful house that the neighbors see doesn't always match what is going on behind closed doors. You felt puzzled about yourself and thought, *No one understands me* or *No one likes me*.

Growing up in a mid-range intensity household indicates that your childhood was not filled with big emotional or traumatic events that happened over and over, but at times the family could tip over into bad times. This is a childhood in which the hurtful or angry times could overshadow the happy times. There were adults who you felt were safe and in charge, but there were also those who frightened you, and you tried to stay away from them.

In a mid-range intensity household, alcohol, drugs, gambling, and other addictions may show up in parents, siblings, or other relatives.

How a mid-range intensity household experience may manifest in adult life

You came away from this type of childhood feeling more battle-scarred than your friends but generally OK. You feel good about yourself most of the time. You may take or have taken medications or therapy for anxiety or depression in your adult life, but this is, for the most part, not an ongoing need. You may be able to stay in a long-term relationship, but it will require work to make it functional, as many of your unresolved issues from childhood will be brought into your adult relationships.

HIGH-INTENSITY HOUSEHOLD

An overall high-intensity household indicates a childhood with consistent turmoil and upset. There may have been stable adults around, but this was not a constant. You were always searching for someone in charge, and if you couldn't find a grounded adult, then you felt like you had to be in charge and stay in control because everyone else was out of control. You often had physical issues such as headaches, gut issues, nervousness, and being hypervigilant. This watchful feeling would happen even when things were good because you were always waiting for the next explosion to happen.

Chaos, alcohol abuse, and multiple addictions by the parents or primary caregivers are often seen in this type of household. The caregivers were often lost in their own troubles and didn't have time for you. The first-born became super responsible, or the kids all checked out and looked for ways to escape.

How a high-intensity household experience may manifest in adult life

As an adult, you have tried therapy multiple times and have been on and off different types of medications in your desire to feel better. Your early life and adult life are confusing to you, and you wonder how other people are able to be happy. You have difficulty maintaining emotionally close connections with your partners, and you are drawn to the same type of person over and over even though you know they are not good for you. You may say you don't want the type of household you had growing up, but it seems like chaos is inevitable.

Recall my story, for example. I rated my age of wounding at ten years old, and rated my traumatic memory of getting my sister and myself to safety as high in intensity, at a level 10. I evaluated that my childhood family experience went from the mid- to high-intensity household range.

EXERCISE: CHILDHOOD HOUSEHOLD INTENSITY PATTERNS

Look over your timeline, your intensity ratings, and these household descriptions. What patterns do you see were in your childhood household?

_____

Do you see your childhood household experience from a different perspective now? How would you describe your childhood household?

_____

_____

_____

These intensity ratings help to illustrate and quantify your experiences so you can be objective with your own history. I include them as reference points so you know that you are not alone, that many others come from similar experiences.

You have been doing some difficult searching inside, probably looking at things you haven't thought about for a long time. At times this emotional excavation is really heavy, tiring, and overwhelming. We will continue to go even deeper, but for now, let's take a short break and give your emotions a rest.

EXERCISE: YOUR TREASURE CHEST

Our emotional treasures don't always sparkle.

I want to teach you a meditation and visualization technique that is useful for when you bring up emotionally heavy parts of your past, as you did in the last exercise.

Picture all of the things you have been thinking about from your childhood, all of the emotional wounding events that are in your conscious mind. Imagine these events scattered on the floor like little treasures. As you begin to connect to them, remember that you are discovering a lot of emotion that is packed within each situation.

Picture a treasure chest on the floor along with all of your scattered childhood memories. The treasure chest is the safe cocoon that will hold all of these emotionally laden events so you don't feel like you are walking around open and exposed, raw with emotion. It will magically expand to hold everything you will be putting into it.

Pick up and hold a memory, and thank it for being in your life. Even if it was painful to go through when you were younger, it is still a treasured part of you because all of you is treasured. Hold this memory, thank it, and place it in the treasure chest.

Continue to put your emotional memories into the treasure chest one by one until you have gathered them all. Once they are all in the chest, close the lid.

Put this treasure chest in a safe place inside of you. Know that when the time is right you will open it and gently bring out these emotional memories. In time, you will be healing the emotions that are wrapped around each of the more painful events, but for now, keep them in a safe place so you can begin to feel whole again as you do this healing work.

Emotional Standouts

Look at your timeline again and note the events that you rated between 7 and 10 on the Emotional Response Scale. These are the emotional standouts that have a high emotional intensity, the experiences that were difficult for you and impacted your life path. When you are triggered or remember these standouts, you remember them very clearly, and they really hurt. Use a highlighter to mark these emotional standouts on your timeline.

EXERCISE: YOUR EMOTIONAL STANDOUTS

In the space below, write out the emotional standouts from your timeline. If there are a lot, what are the themes or patterns you see with these emotional standouts? If your entire childhood was of high emotional intensity, what is the theme or feeling you had during most of your childhood?

_____

_____

_____

_____

Your Age of Wounding

In earlier chapters in the book, we touched on the age of wounding, a dramatic or emotionally significant event you experienced as a child that resulted in a core wounding. This wounding event gets linked with the age you were when it occurred, which results in the wounding becoming frozen in time, trapped in a snow globe within you.

EXERCISE: DETERMINING YOUR AGE OF WOUNDING

What is your age of wounding? Do you have more than one age of wounding that shows up in your timeline? In the space below, look over your emotional standouts and the age for each, then look at your intensity rating for those standouts. Are there one or two ages where things were really hard for you as a child?

In the space below, write out the age you were when the wounding happened and what the wounding was. To the right of the age, write down the effects that this wounding had on you. How did this wounding experience change or shape how you looked at yourself or others? Don't overthink this exercise; you have done a lot of work to prepare yourself to discover your age of wounding. Identifying your age of wounding will establish your connection with your lost inner child.

Did you have more than one age of wounding? Having more than one age of wounding is not uncommon, but for now, choose one that you would like to focus on as you complete the exercises later in the workbook.

EXERCISE: SIMPLE BREATHING

You are doing a lot of hard work here. This simple breath exercise helps to rebalance your system and tells all parts of you that you are safe and there is no need to feel scared. Looking out at nature or listening to some relaxing music adds to the experience. Give yourself this gift of gentle breathing.

Sit comfortably in a quiet place. Close your eyes, place one hand on your belly, and take a long, slow breath in through your nose, then gently exhale through your mouth. Don't force it, just breathe gently in through your nose and out through your mouth, as if you were gently blowing out a candle. At first you may breathe faster than you need to, but just relax into the flow and go slowly. Do this exercise for as long as you like, and frequently throughout the day, to balance your system.

Identifying Your Triggers

Look over the list of wounded emotional response tools that you identified in "Exercise: Your Impulsive Response Tools" in chapter 1. Use this list to help you identify some of your triggers.

EXERCISE: IDENTIFYING YOUR TRIGGERS

Think about a situation that upsets you, then write down your answers to the following questions. Don't overthink your answers to these questions. Your first instinct is usually your hotline to your subconscious.

When and where does this situation usually happen?

_____

Is this a sight, sound, smell, touch, or memory?

_____

Is your trigger a person, a thing, or a situation?

_____

How often does it occur?

_____

What are some immediate feelings you have when this situation occurs? (I immediately feel . . .)

_____

Where do you feel this in your body?

_____

Do you find you want to say or do something, or do you want to be super quiet and withdraw?

_____

Are the same people or same type of people involved in this situation?

_____

Who or what does this situation remind you of from your early life?

_____

Do you notice any patterns or themes that stand out in your answers? How do your answers here compare to the other exercises you have completed? You are developing more of an understanding of how, when, and why you respond the way you do in certain situations. You are getting to know yourself in a deeper way.

Now look over your answers from "Exercise: Your Impulsive Response Tools" again, and think about what happens when you use these impulsive reactions. In the spaces below, write down a trigger that precedes each impulsive reaction. What are the situations or things that prompt your impulsive reaction response? Do you self-sabotage, avoid, or lash out? For example, self-sabotage may be connected to the trigger of feeling like someone is criticizing you. If you lash out, the trigger could be the feeling of not being heard. This is another way to determine some of your triggers. Write out as many as you can think of.

I'm triggered by:

_____

_____

I impulsively react by:

_____

_____

Later I feel:

_____

_____

Writing Healing Letters to Yourself

Writing healing letters to and from yourself is a great way to immediately get feelings out and connect to that wounded part of yourself. These letters are written in a stream-of-consciousness style, that is, fast and without editing or judging. With this style of writing, you sit down and get it all out without overthinking or pre-thinking what you are going to write. That inner wounding is looking to be heard and acknowledged, and this process is a helpful and efficient way to do so. These letters are meant just for you.

The main goal in writing these letters is to connect to the frozen part of you that carries the age of wounding. Once you form this connection you will begin to see, hear, and feel how your wounding shows up in your adult life. The letters will create a bridge that will bring your frozen wounding into the light of day.

The process sounds simple, and it is, yet it does many things all at once and works on many levels. After you have written the first letters, you will be able to connect to your feelings in a different way than when you just think about or express the thoughts verbally. You will be giving yourself permission to fully and freely express emotions that have been bottled up or unexpressed for a long time. Letter writing provides a safe outlet for this contained and bottled-up energy.

Putting pen to paper accesses a deep part of us. The kinetic movement forms a bridge between the conscious and the subconscious. When we use our fine motor skills to write out our feelings, we are giving the heart a pathway to release pent-up emotion. Once we put our thoughts and feeling onto paper, we can face them and learn how to hold them in a new way. This takes tremendous courage, which is why people will put off doing this simple exercise. However, you have come this far in the process and can no longer deny that events happened in childhood that affect you as an adult.

Please remember that these letters are a form of focused writing. They are not meant for anyone other than you. Please keep them for now, as you will look back over them when you get to your integration later in the HEAL process.

Letter from Your Younger Self to Your Adult Self

The first letter you write will be from a younger wounded part of you to your adult self. The goal of this letter writing exchange is to bring into the light of day the pain, confusion, misunderstanding, distortion, and false narrative that the younger self carries. After all, it is this lack of perspective that keeps the younger self stuck and always on guard. This letter exchange is designed to clearly state what those issues are and spell out how they got that way. The responsible adult self then has the opportunity to respond, clear up misconceptions, and give the younger self the love, validation, trust, and respect that it has never have had before.

Find a quiet place to do this work. If you can't find a quiet place at home, be creative. Is there a secluded place or backyard you can sit in for privacy? Before you start writing, read through the instructions so you won't have to stop in the middle of writing.

Look over your timeline, and identify the specific age of wounding and the event that you are ready to write about. Close your eyes and begin to ask that wounded part to describe how they feel. Begin to connect with your wounded and lost inner child. The following questions can help you visualize the setting.

How old is this part of you?

What was going on in the household?

_____

Who was there?

_____

What did it feel, sound, and smell like?

_____

What was happening?

_____

What you were feeling?

_____

What are the secrets this part has been holding on to?

_____

What are the deep, heavy hurts this part carries?

_____

What does your child self want to say to your responsible adult self?

When you are ready, start writing in the full-page blank space. Don't think about it, just write. Keep pushing your pen or pencil to move, and let out whatever comes. It doesn't have to make sense, and you don't even have to be able to read it. Write fast and furious; don't edit or worry about good penmanship. Be in the flow of the moment. (Sometimes people ask if they can type their letter, and certainly that works, but there is a difference between the two modalities. Try both ways to see which one gives you deeper results.)

Transfer your feelings and thoughts onto the paper. Write for as long as it takes. Don't stop until you feel you have said what you want to say. If there is more inside of you, keep going until you can't think of another thing your wounded part wants or needs to say.

Don't rush through the exercise or think you have to quickly move ahead to the next part of the process. Be gentle with yourself right now; pushing yourself through the work is not going to heal you faster.

EXERCISE: LETTER FROM MY YOUNGER SELF
TO MY ADULT SELF

Letter from Your Adult Self to Your Younger Self

Now you are ready for your adult self to connect with your younger self. Ideally, your adult self will be loving, caring, and nurturing. After all, you just read all of the painful emotions that your younger self has been holding on to for so many years.

As you learned in the book, your responsible adult self is the part of you that has matured, pays the bills, and does the work of being an adult in the world. It is your grounded part. Your younger self needs to hear from your protective, responsible adult self that you will set strong boundaries, and that you can handle whatever it was that created the woundings and triggers in the first place. If the younger self doesn't believe you, or if you do not create strong boundaries, then the younger self will not put down its wounded emotional response tools.

Things to remember:

- Acknowledge all of the pain and wounding that this part carries, and validate specific feelings from that time.
- Let this part know that you will not abandon or ignore it until it is healed and integrated with your adult self.
- State that you will protect all parts of your wounded inner child by establishing strong boundaries for yourself and others.

EXERCISE: LETTER FROM YOUR ADULT SELF
TO YOUR YOUNGER SELF

Look back over the healing letters you just wrote. How does it feel to address those feelings and to give them a voice? How does it feel to let your inner child finally be able to acknowledge and put the truth out there that has been in the shadows for so long? How does it feel to give love, kindness, and nurturing from your adult self to your younger self?

This is tremendous work that you are doing. Writing these letters is a key part of the HEAL process. You will probably need to write a number of letters back and forth to bring out the emotion and then process all of these complex feelings you have carried over the years.

Be patient with yourself as you do this work. It is not a one-and-done kind of experience. It is a dynamic, transformational process that takes you into a deeper level of yourself.

The goal of the letter writing is for you to begin to understand the voice and the feelings that your lost inner child carries. You are doing this work now so that you can develop a dialogue with your younger self and thus know when it is starting to become triggered and wanting to step in front of the adult self to defend you.

Developing Functional Tools to Manage Triggering Events

This exercise will help you to identify more clearly where each trigger came from, what it needs in order to heal, and how to make a plan for using functional tools.

EXERCISE: MANAGING TRIGGERS

Review the list of triggers you wrote down in the exercise titled "Identify Your Triggers" earlier in the workbook. Next to each trigger, write down where that trigger came from and what it needs in order to heal. For example:

Trigger: Being disrespected. This trigger really bothers me. It comes from never feeling heard or valued. This part needs to be honored and heard, and I need to set stronger boundaries with people.

Once you have identified the source of a trigger, come up with a plan for your responsible adult self to remain in charge. For example, you can make an agreement with the younger wounded part that you are going to be proactive and take care of all of this wounding now that you have a good idea of where your triggers come from, what they are, what your impulsive reactions are to your triggers, and what you want to do to heal this cycle. You are building a set of functional response tools to add to your toolbox.

This trigger list and your functional response toolbox will help your adult self remember what you need to do to take care of yourself emotionally every day. The more you consciously work on developing new functional tools and addressing your triggers each day, the sooner you will shift out of the dysfunctional dance with your wounding. This is a daily practice that you will need to remind yourself to do at first, but once you get in the habit, it will feel natural.

In the space below, write down your triggers and what they need to heal so they are no longer activated.

EXERCISES FROM CHAPTER 6
BOUNDARIES

You learned a lot about boundaries in chapter 6 in the book. The exercises in this section will help you to determine where your boundaries are, how strong they are, and whether they are internal or external.

Internal Boundaries

The following are examples of internal boundary statements. Which ones do you connect to more than others?

- I am not going to go to the bar with my friends because I know that environment is not good for me.
- I am not going to yell, scream, demand, deceive, blame, ridicule, or demean others.
- I am not going to take in the criticisms of others.
- I am going to be honest and vulnerable with myself.
- I am going to honor myself today and not beat up on myself if I make a mistake.
- I am going to keep my commitment to myself and go to the gym at least twice a week.
- I am going to find a therapist to help me with my depression and anxiety.
- I am going to maintain strong boundaries with others and say no when I need to.
- I am going to keep a gratitude journal of all the things that I am grateful for each day.
- I am going to smile more and practice finding the good in myself and others.

These boundaries are examples of making commitments to oneself and how to honor and respect those commitments. People who know themselves have a strong internal boundary system. People who look to others to define their world often have fuzzy internal boundaries and are all over the place when it comes to decision making. They give others the power to define their internal reality and identity.

EXERCISE: INTERNAL BOUNDARY COMMITMENTS

Write out some internal boundary commitments you use or would like to make for yourself:

External Boundaries

External boundaries are statements or positions you establish with another person or situation. These boundaries are in place when you have clarity internally about what you want or don't want and then express this clarity to another person in simple, clear, and assertive statements. External boundaries are often in the form of "I" statements. For example:

- I feel hurt that you didn't include me.
- I feel that my personal space is being disrespected. I don't like it when you stand so close to me. Can you step back?
- I feel confused about why you don't ask me for help.
- I feel hurt because of the way you continually talk down to me.
- I feel trusting and safe in our relationship.
- I feel excited that you are taking me on the trip with you.
- I feel great gratitude and joy that you are my friend. Thank you for being in my life.
- I am going to respect you and your personal property by not snooping or listening in, and I ask for the same from you (internal and external boundaries).
- I feel uncomfortable doing what you want me to do sexually.
- I will be respectful of you and will try not to control you.
- I will respect you when you say no, and I ask you to respect me when I say no.

EXERCISE: EXTERNAL BOUNDARY STATEMENTS

Internal and external boundary statements are not always about saying no. They can also state what you will do or agree to. Write down some external boundary statements you need to make in your life today:

Making "I" Statements

When you make a boundary statement, it is important to make it an "I" statement. Boundary statements are not about blaming or shaming someone else, as in, "You made me angry. You are always doing this, and you never do that." The "I" statement is designed to help the other person be less defensive and thus able to hear your feelings.

To set a healthy boundary, check in with yourself in the moment and ask, *How do I feel about this person, place, or situation right now?* Your boundary statement is your gut reaction. You will have a physical reaction somewhere in your body if this idea feels good to you or not. Be careful not to override this reaction and start making excuses for the other person's behavior.

If you make up stories, this is your wounding showing up and saying you shouldn't set a boundary. *Well, he has had a hard time of it*, or, *I'll go ahead and do this for him*, or, *I don't always want to say no to her because if I do, she's not going to like me.* Most people who struggle with saying no to others do so because they don't want to offend, don't want to get into it, or are people pleasers and conflict avoiders. People who have the hardest time learning to set boundaries are those who talk themselves out of the boundary in the first place. The rule to remember is, if you don't want to do something, if you don't like something, if you don't need something, then say no. Use your discernment to figure out how you want to set your boundary.

It is harder to set boundaries in relationships that have meaning to us because we have more invested in these relationships and more to lose. Trust yourself and the relationship to hold your boundary. Any relationship worth having and developing is going to have a healthy boundary exchange. Someone who doesn't respect your boundaries usually will not have a good boundary system themselves, and chances are they are narcissistically inclined.

We often have better boundaries in professional settings because there are defined rules and we clearly know what is our work to do and what is someone else's. Most people have a good boundary sense at work, but when many people get home, that boundary sense goes away. Most people tell me that they can set boundaries at work but not at home, so they are aware of their boundary skills. But in their intimate relationships they don't want to seem controlling, pushy, or mean. Functional boundary setting is not any of those things.

Boundary violations occur when our boundaries are not honored or respected. We can also violate or go against our own boundary by ignoring or pushing aside how we feel or what we mean to say.

EXERCISE: PRACTICE "I" STATEMENTS

In the space below, write out two or three "I" statements for practice. Don't overthink it, just put the feeling down after you write "I."

_____

_____

_____

_____

Choosing Healthy Boundaries

Let's look at some specific healthy boundaries that you can start to practice right now.

EXERCISE: PRACTICING HEALTHY BOUNDARIES

First review your answers to "Exercise: Your Impulsive Response Tools" in chapter 1. Then find the items that best match your impulsive reactions in the following list. Note the healthy boundary response that goes with each one. Pick one or two specific healthy boundaries that relate to your wounding, and start practicing. Which of the following statements and affirmations do you think you need to follow? Why? If you connect to one more deeply than another, practice saying it out loud, and notice how it feels.

- If you give away your power, the healthy response is to look at ways to pull it back in. Affirm: *I am in charge of my personal power and will not turn it over to someone else.*
- If you say yes so that someone else won't be angry, then practice saying small no's. Let the other person feel their own feelings. Affirm: *It is OK for me to say no and for other people to have their own feelings.*
- If you try to control others, ask yourself what you don't trust. Then affirm: *I am in the flow of life, and I am my authentic self with others.*
- If you try to manipulate others, ask yourself what you don't trust. Look at your internal boundaries. Affirm: *I trust in myself and others.*
- If you test others, ask yourself what parts of yourself you don't love. Affirm: *I am learning to love myself.*

- If you play the victim, ask yourself if it is for attention. What is this really about? Affirm: *I am learning to validate and accept all parts of myself. I take responsibility for myself.*
- If you overcompensate and keep doing for others, then look at ways to increase your self-love and just be instead of do. Affirm: *I am more than enough.*
- If you push someone away with the hope of starting anew with someone else instead of working on your relationship issues, ask yourself if this is a familiar pattern and if it is worth going through the cycle all over again. Affirm: *I am finding the courage to look at those parts of myself that are difficult to see.*
- If you have low self-esteem, think of one thing a day you are proud of or that you did well, and express that to yourself. Affirm: *Each day I am proud of my grounded choices.*
- If you do not speak your truth, think of how you can honor yourself by speaking words that reflect who you are today. Affirm: *It is easier to speak the truth than to clean up many untruths.*
- If you make yourself smaller to fit into someone else's world, gently stand up tall, take a deep breath, and know you are worthy of feeling your full power. Reclaim your worth.

Many of these healthy responses set and affirm internal boundaries. These internal boundary statements are what you say to yourself in quiet moments. You can work on replenishing your self-worth and self-love by practicing these statements, which will help to heal your wounded inner child and reinforce your boundary setting.

Bubble Boundaries

Many people walk around with an emotional suit of armor on, prepared at all times for an imaginary battle. The wounded part of them doesn't know that the battle is over, so they suit up every day with their wounded burden. They have what I call a "bubble boundary" around them to protect themselves from the world.

A bubble boundary is strong but fragile, malleable but rigid. It is the boundary you have when you hold people at arm's length, when you feel simultaneously guarded and open. It is neither extreme nor enmeshed. You participate in life and enjoy being with other people, yet you clench your teeth hoping they don't get too close. When you are in your bubble you feel protected; you can still see others and even let them get close, but you know in a millisecond when they get too close and touch your bubble boundary. Your bubble boundary is your sanctuary.

People with bubble boundaries learned to protect themselves from a childhood family where attacks came in the form of sly, passive-aggressive comments or deafening silence. There may have been very little expression or modeling of emotion in the household, so they never learned how to show their feelings.

Because of this lack of healthy emotional availability, these children grow up emotionally neglected and make up stories to make sense of their world. Basic needs such as food, clothing, and shelter were met, but emotional nourishment and nurturing went unfulfilled.

EXERCISE: BUBBLE WITH A WINDOW

This exercise will help you to evaluate your layers of protection and see how you keep yourself safe inside your bubble and keep others out. You can start building deeper connections with others by opening a window in your bubble.

Review your answers to "Exercise: Your Impulsive Response Tools" in chapter 1. These tools reveal where you need a better sense of internal and external boundaries. This exercise is designed to help you recognize what you are doing when you are doing it so you can gain new perspective on yourself.

In figure 2 you will see a large circle that represents your bubble boundary. The inside of the bubble is how you feel and what you say to yourself, and the outside is your interactions with others, what you say and how you behave. Your bubble has a window that opens to your outside world. You can connect with others through this window, but it is also how you lock them out. As you work through this exercise, you will look at when, where, and why you want connection with others and when you shut them out.

Inside the bubble, write down what you tell yourself that keeps the window closed and yourself isolated. These are the reasons you have the bubble boundary, the purpose it serves. For example, you might write down feelings of being scared, frightened, hurt, lonely, and confused. You could write your thoughts and actions that reinforce a victim narrative, such as *I'm not good enough*, *It's not worth it, I'm never going to find anyone*, and *I'm always rejected*. For example, perhaps you promise to give up trying to find a partner, believe that deeply connecting with someone else is too risky, or are tired of being vulnerable with others because they don't share anything with you. Or maybe you blame others, feel victimized, or are tired of the rejection. You can also write feeling words or expressions that you say to yourself over and over. (See table 1, the Feelings Chart, in the introduction for feeling words.)

Everything you put outside the bubble either expands and connects you or contracts and isolates you. At the top and outside of the bubble, write down what your interactions look like when the window is open and you are connected to others. How do you interact? What do you say? These are actions and things you say when you feel safe and trusting of others enough to reach outside your bubble. Write down the qualities of what it takes for you to trust and connect to others, such as, *I can be myself around my good friends, I trust this type of person*, and *I feel safe when I go to this person's house or this kind of gathering*. These items expand you and open you up to bring others into your life.

Next, at the bottom and outside of the bubble, write down what your interactions look like when the window is closed. These are the actions you take and what you say to keep people at arm's length. Do you avoid situations in which you have to talk with others? Do you talk only to "safe" people? Do you give people mixed messages? Are you noncommittal by using phrases such as, "I don't know if I can, let me see," or "Maybe"? Do you say you will do something and then back out at the last minute? How does your wounding and bubble boundary show up in your relationships? You can also write down people, places, and situations you avoid because they are too much work or they scare you. These words or actions contract and limit you, and reinforce that others should stay away, keeping you isolated.

FIGURE 2: BUBBLE BOUNDARY CIRCLE

BUBBLE BOUNDARY ASSESSMENT

Once you have identified how you behave and think outside and inside your bubble, ask yourself the following questions. Write down your answers to the questions that are relevant to you.

Do I still need to say these things to others to keep myself safe?

_____

What purpose does my bubble boundary serve? Do I just keep it out of habit?

_____

Am I truly unsafe in my connections with others, or am I overgeneralizing and unsure of my next steps?

_____

Do I keep people out of my bubble because I am afraid and don't want to be hurt again?

_____

Am I ready to welcome people into my life, or do I want to keep shutting them out?

_____

Do I still need to say these mean things to myself? How does this help me?

_____

What do I need to do to heal the negative messages I tell myself?

_____

What do I think is going to happen if I learn to set healthy boundaries and have my bubble window open more?

_____

How do these messages relate to my age of wounding?

_____

Is this a new age of wounding showing up?

_____

Do I give myself or others mixed messages?

_____

What do I say to others that gives them the impression that I want to stay inside my bubble?

_____

How do I feel when I look at the people and situations I trust when my bubble window is open?

_____

How do I feel when I look at the people and situations I don't trust when my bubble window is closed?

_____

Why do I close my window and not let others in?

_____

How can I get clarity with my boundary setting with others so I feel safer?

_____

How can I set better internal boundaries to be safe as an option to staying isolated?

_____

Once I am clear with my internal boundaries, what are some small steps I can take to open myself up to others?

_____

_____

Understanding why and how you keep others out when you really want to feel closeness will help you discern what you want to do with your bubble boundary. You have a choice in how you interact with yourself and life. You don't have to continue to keep other people out as a form of protection. This is not about popping your bubble and not having any protection; learning to set healthy, functional boundaries can replace your home-grown bubble boundary approach and help you feel authentically whole.

If you want to open your bubble window and deepen a relationship with another, choose someone who will receive this information with love and respect. Don't make a big production of having this conversation. You could simply say, "I've been meaning to share something with you," or "I want to talk about something that is hard for me to say, but I want to share it with you." Chances are they probably want a deeper connection as well. With this approach you establish an internal boundary of what is OK and not OK to share with them, and you invite them to know you on a deeper level. You are communicating that you want to be more open with them and hope that they can share more openly with you. It is an invitation for a deeper connection, which is a basic need for most people.

Remember that you are responsible only for yourself and cannot control or change anyone else, so however they respond to your sharing is their choice. The most important part of this process is that you are giving yourself permission to break the cycle of being guarded with others when you don't need to be. You are giving yourself the opportunity to experience emotional freedom in your relationships. However the conversation turns out, congratulate yourself for using boundaries and functional ways of expressing yourself to share a part of yourself. You are learning how to open up. You are learning to become emotionally available to yourself and others.

Sometimes Setting Boundaries Is Hard

Let's go a little deeper with some questions about why you have a difficult time setting boundaries. Look over these questions and go a little deeper within yourself. See if you can discern why you are this way with some people and not with others. Go with the first thing that pops in your head, and answer the question without editing or getting in the way of yourself. Be as honest as you can with yourself. Remember, this work is just for you unless you wish to share it.

Have I tried to have a sense of power or to set boundaries in my relationships but gave up when it didn't work? (They didn't like me saying no, so this didn't work. I will just agree with them from now on.)

_____

Do I have a sense of whether people are good for me or toxic? Is it hard for me to see the distinction?

_____

Have I honestly examined whether or not I play the victim role in my relationships? (Poor me.)

_____

Do I blame others or the situation and avoid taking responsibility for my actions?

_____

Do I know what is important to me, or do I just follow the leader and those who I think are better than me?

_____

Do I just want everybody to get along and not get into all of this drama? (Magical thinking.)

_____

Am I concerned that if I set boundaries, some people will not want to be in a relationship with me because I no longer cater to them?

_____

Have I created a list of my wants and needs?

_____

Have I actively tried taking care of myself?

_____

Have I honestly tried to not be involved in someone else's life as a distraction to my own? (Am I preoccupied with others so I don't have to look at myself?)

_____

Your answers to these questions will help you begin to look at the patterns and themes that repeatedly show up in your life. If you need help creating a list of your needs, please see table 2, the Needs Inventory, in the introduction.

Extreme Boundaries

Extreme boundaries are the opposite of no boundaries and are much harsher than bubble boundaries. An extreme boundary involves making a dramatic life change that an individual believes is the only way they can keep themselves emotionally, physical, mentally, or sexually safe from another person. An example of an extreme boundary is when the individual moves to a different state or country to get away from another person or a family. Constructing such a boundary is like building a reinforced concrete fortress: it will keep others out for good.

People who establish extreme boundaries are usually angry and hurt from something someone did to them, or they feel a great deal of fear about something. They are willing to walk away from a friendship, relationship, or work environment as a response to the fear they feel. They perceive that there are no other alternatives and that the only way to protect themselves is to shut out the other person or situation. Most people, however, establish extreme boundaries too quickly and out of a sense of frustration rather than a fear of being harmed. This happens when they don't know how to establish healthy boundaries.

Some examples of extreme boundaries are:

- I am moving away and not telling you where I am going.
- I am blocking you from all contact, including phone and social media.

- I won't acknowledge you even when we are in the same room.
- I will say no to everything and shut out everyone.
- I am not going to acknowledge my pain. I will shut myself off from myself. (This is an example of an extreme internal boundary.)

Some of these extreme nonfunctional boundaries sound like they would be set by someone who needs to move a thousand miles away for their own protection, and some people do need to move away or block someone from their life for their own safety. (If this is the case for you, please see Resources in appendix C in the book.) However, extreme boundaries need to be carefully considered and are a last resort because of the potential long-term damage they can create in a relationship connection.

If you are tempted to create an extreme boundary with someone in your life, ask yourself the following questions to determine whether this is the best option for you.

Before you set an extreme boundary, ask yourself:

Have I examined my feelings from a place of being grounded and not overly emotional?

How do I feel as a result of what this person did or is doing to me?

Do I need to set an extreme boundary, or is there a functional boundary I can establish?

Have I expressed my boundaries with this person?

Have I tried multiple times to engage with them or to meet up emotionally and talk things through?

Have I tried my best to make this work with functional boundaries?

Do I feel that no matter how clearly I express my boundaries, the other person does not respect them?

Do I feel abused and neglected?

Are my needs not being heard or respected?

Have I considered the consequences of setting an extreme boundary with this person?

How will I feel after I set an extreme boundary?

What will the ramifications be on attempts to repair this relationship in the future?

Do I have a clear sense of the other person's position?

Am I making assumptions based on what they do or on what they say they feel?

Do I feel threatened in any way? If so, do I need to set an extreme boundary for my own safety and that of my family?

Are my boundaries continually violated no matter what I say or do?

If you have answered these questions from a place of grounded clarity and still feel that you need an extreme boundary for personal and family protection, then proceed with caution and care. If you start to feel anger, spite, revenge, jealousy, and rage, then take a moment to re-center yourself. After you feel calmer, ask yourself if you need an extreme boundary or just need to work through your feelings. You want to feel grounded and centered when making such decision.

Bonus Content: Boundaries at Work and Home

Boundaries are so important as part of your healing process that I have included bonus content so you can go deeper into the topic. As you have already done boundary exercises, you know that most people have some kind of boundary system that they use to create a sense of personal space and agency. These systems are not always functional, but they work at some level to create emotional guardrails in relationships.

Recall that internal boundaries are commitments or promises you make to yourself privately, and external boundaries are statements you make to others so they know how you feel about a certain situation. In this section you will examine different aspects of your life to determine where you are doing a good job at boundary setting and where you need some boundary remediation.

BOUNDARIES IN THE WORKPLACE

Let's start with your boundaries in your workplace. I like to start here because people often have better boundaries at work than they have anywhere else in their lives. I believe this is because there are clearly defined boundaries at work; you know your job, and you know what other people's jobs are. There is usually a manager, a boss, and some kind of human resources department that holds the workplace boundaries intact. The management of the company establishes the boundary rules for the workplace and enforces these rules of company conduct, behavior, morals, and ethics.

Just as in childhood families with parents who have poor boundaries, when management has poor boundaries, the entire workplace is affected. Perhaps you are or have been at a workplace where the manager or business owner has poor boundaries. There are often poor relations between departments, with backstabbing, passive-aggressiveness, and implicit permission for employees and managers alike to show their emotional wounding by letting it spill out onto everyone else. In other words, it is a big dysfunctional family in which everyone is expected to play their role—and collect a paycheck.

This is a toxic workplace environment. It developed to this point because management at the top did not see or recognize that the lack of boundaries was a problem, and because they themselves often have poor boundaries.

Beverly, who comes to see me, had developed friendships with a few of her coworkers. When she first started working on her healing, she talked about all the fun things she did with her friends, both at work and outside of work. She would speak of them in glowing terms, talking about things they were doing together and what they were interested in.

As time went on and her inner child healed, she began to notice that a couple of her friends did not speak very kindly to her. She saw how they were critical of her and talked behind her back. As Beverly became emotionally healthier, she realized that this was how they had always spoken to her and about her. When she confronted one of her friends with a boundary statement that she felt hurt by how she was spoken to, her friend turned her words back on her and blamed her for what she was doing.

Beverly no longer shares outside experiences with these women. They still work together, though she has placed clear boundaries to protect herself from their hurtful comments and behaviors. She is still friendly with them at work, but she said that realizing how they spoke to her hurt, because she thought she knew them. The other women didn't change, but she did.

BONUS EXERCISE: BOUNDARIES AT WORK

Consider your workplace, your coworkers, your friends at work, and the work environment in general. This exercise will help you think about the boundaries that are in place, and notice how they help you or work against you. You may be able to determine how, when, why, and where your inner child shows up in your workplace.

Complete the following statements:

I am able to have good boundaries at work because:

_____

I am encouraged to use boundaries at work by (a person or policy):

_____

I like the workplace boundaries, and I feel _____ knowing they are in place.

I struggle at times with boundaries at work with or because of (person or policy):

_____

My workplace boundaries are stronger than other boundaries because:

_____

I have a stronger voice at work than I do at home because:

_____

My boundaries at work are challenged all the time by this person:

_____

My boundaries at work are violated in the following ways:

_____

I have tried to talk with this person about how they violate my boundaries, but:

_____

I notice that others have the same problem, and I see them do this:

_____

I make myself smaller at work because:

_____

I give in to other people at work because:

_____

I can't be myself at work because:

_____

I avoid conflict at work because:

_____

When I am at work, I wish that I could:

_____

I don't want others to see that I feel:

_____

My inner child shows up at work with these people and situations:

_____

If I could, I would tell this person: _____
that I am:

_____

I can't express my feelings at work, but sometimes I would like to say:

_____

When this person: _____ does this thing:_____
I feel:_____

I wish that I could just go in and do my job, but:

_____

My boss or coworkers remind me of the emotional dramas I had with _____ in my personal life.

I see these patterns at work that also happen in my personal life:

_____

My three main inner child triggers that are activated at work are:

1)

2)

3)

When I am triggered at work, I realize these issues didn't start at work, they started:

_____

When I am triggered at work, I know I can control my reactions if I:

_____

No matter what I do or say, this keeps happening:

_____

This person gives me the most trouble.at work:

This person who I am triggered by reminds me of:

I wish I could tell this triggering person to:

_____

When I have tried to tell this person what I feel, they:

_____

I have learned to avoid this person, but doing so makes me feel:

_____

If I could change the relationship dynamic with this person, I would:

_____

If this situation were changed:_____

I would feel:_____

I know I can't control or change other people, so I need to look at this part of my own life:

_____

I don't want to have to work so hard at my work relationships, but:

_____

I like my job; I just don't like:

_____

After exploring my feelings about workplace boundaries, I now see that:

_____

So that I am not triggered as much at work, I will continue to heal this inner wound:

_____

I need to do a better job of setting healthy boundaries at work with these people:

_____

To do this, I need to do the following:

_____

The main people I need to set boundaries with at work are:

_____

When I am at work, I need to tell my inner child this:

_____

BOUNDARIES WITH FRIENDS AND FAMILY

Establishing and maintaining healthy boundaries in our personal lives is often harder than doing so at work. Most of us use the boundaries that we saw our parents use, and we repeat their patterns of behavior. Boundaries create a sense of safety in our personal lives, although, as you have learned, without a strong boundary system, relationships can quickly become emotionally messy.

As you heal and set boundaries, you may notice that you don't feel as connected to friends or family as you once did. Essentially, as you heal you will expand your idea of yourself and recognize who is good for you and who is bad or toxic for you. I have seen this in my own life. As I grew into understanding and healing myself, I didn't want to be around some of my more manipulative friends. I began to see them for who they were instead of who I needed them to be to complete my dysfunctional drama. Parts of me were healing, and I could see how they treated me, how they talked to me, and that they were not honoring or respectful.

This aspect of healing may be hard for you, as a part of you probably wants to continue toxic friendships, especially if you have known someone for a long time. But as the smokescreen clears, you can't avoid realizing that this person isn't good for you, or that you don't feel good when you are around that person. You thought you knew who they were, but you may go through a gradual *aha!* process and see them for who they really are. When this happens, you may wonder if they have always been this way (they have) and how you didn't see it.

Your wounded part chose dysfunctional friends because doing so made sense. This wounded part meshed with their wounded part, so you thought it was a functional match. Your wounded part needed those toxic friends to complete part of your wounding story, but the healed part of you doesn't want anything to do with them anymore.

Remember to be gentle with yourself as you go through this process of unfolding and self-awareness. You do not have to wholesale clean house and get rid of everyone in your life because you see how toxic they are. Instead, set boundaries with friends who you now see are controlling or manipulative. If they honor your boundary statements and respect your attempt to make the relationship more functional, including your saying no, great. But if not, then it may be time to move on.

Specific people in your group of friends are usually there because you have mutual interests, you connect on many views and outlooks on life, and you feel good when you are around each other. You may keep people in your friend group out of habit, or you may not have anyone else in your life and so will put up with bad behavior on their part. This type of friendship is toxic and not healthy. Many old wounded patterns keep repeating in toxic relationships and friendships. Remember, hurt people find hurt people, and healthy people find healed people.

BONUS EXERCISE: BOUNDARIES WITH FRIENDS AND FAMILY

Consider your friendships and relationships, then complete the following statements to see where, when, how, and why you have strong boundaries, and where having them is hard.

Being myself and setting clear boundaries is easy when I am with:

_____

I am able to be authentic and free with:

_____

When I know I don't like something, I am able to set strong boundaries in these situations:

_____

I have modeled my strong, healthy boundaries on these people in my life:

_____

It is difficult to do, but I know I need to set better boundaries with this person:

_____

I get push-back when I try to set boundaries with this person:

_____

This person disrespects and/or violates my boundaries:_____

When I try to tell this person that they are disrespecting my boundaries, they:

_____

I am confused when they don't respect my boundary, and I start to think this about myself:

_____

Sometimes setting boundaries is difficult because I feel:

_____

Setting boundaries is easiest for me when I feel:

_____

I love my family, but when they don't respect my boundaries, I feel:

_____

When my family tries to talk me out of a boundary, such as trying to change my *no* to a *yes*, I feel:

_____

I avoid this person in my family because they don't respect my boundaries:

_____

When I do say no and mean it, I get _____ from my family.
When other family members set a boundary, their boundary is:

_____

I wish that this family member would hear my needs:

_____

I have tried to tell this family member my needs, but they:

_____

When my boundaries aren't respected, this is what I do to get my needs met:

_____

I try my best to be respectful of other people's boundaries, and I feel this way when they don't respect mine:

_____

If I could, I would tell this person how I feel when they disrespect my boundaries:

_____

I learned boundaries from:

_____

I learned this functional, healthy boundary as a child:

_____

I learned this wounded boundary as a child:

_____

These family members tell me what to do and are too involved in my life:

_____

I don't want to hurt their feelings, but I want to say:

_____

I have tried to hint at this, but they just:

_____

When I am more direct, they:

_____

If only I could say this:

_____

I can be myself around _____ because they are:

_____

When I am with _____ I feel free and open because they will not:

_____

I realize how much this relationship means to me, because when I am with them I feel:

_____

I have kept some of my friends for a long time because:

_____

Even though some of my friends are not good for me and even toxic, I still like them in my life because I feel this way when I am with them:

_____

Considering what I know of my inner child, I realize I keep this person _____
as a friend because they do this for my inner child:

_____

I can see now that this person has the same wounding that this friend or relationship had:

_____

This wounding keeps showing up in my life:

_____

Even though I don't consciously want this, my wounded part keeps attracting this type of person:

_____

I realize now that my wounded inner child needs to know this so that it doesn't keep pulling me
toward that type of person:

_____

These people in my life are a mirror to my wounding:

_____

The struggle you are in today is developing the strength you need for tomorrow.

Three Levels of Communication

There are three levels of information about yourself that you control:

Public: You can share easily identifiable aspects of your life, such as your name, the town you live in, your age, and your occupation. Think of things someone would find on a social media search.

Personal: You can share personal details that you already share with trusted family, friends, and coworkers. These include specific aspects of yourself such as your address, phone number, birthday, favorite band, favorite color, and things you enjoy.

Private: You can share details that you want only close family and friends to know, such as your health status, relationship status, fears, and fantasies. This is information that only a handful of people in your life know about.

Make a list of family, friends, and coworkers, then determine the level of communication you feel safe sharing with each person without overexposing yourself. Next to each person's name, write down the level of communication you have now, and then determine whether this connection feels OK as is or whether you would like to have a deeper level of communication. Most people who are open-hearted in their relationships are at the personal level of communication most of the time and only sometimes share private information.

FAMILY/FRIENDS/COWORKERS   LEVEL OF COMMUNICATION

Healthy, functional boundaries = a healthy, integrated self.

Picket Fence Boundaries

Let's carry this discussion of healthy boundaries even further by using the metaphor of a picket fence. A picket fence creates a physical boundary between properties, and everyone can clearly see which side of the fence each property is on. You can apply this metaphor to a boundary between you and someone else. Imagine a picket fence between you and another person. You can see each other over the fence and through the slats. If the other person were in trouble, you could even jump over this fence to help. The fence creates definition and clearly marks where their space is and where your space is.

The picket fence metaphor is simple, as this type of imagery creates a partition between people and a reminder of the need for healthy boundaries. Learning to create imaginary picket fences as boundaries in your relationships is one of the most mature and responsible actions your adult responsible self can do to care for the wounded parts of you. This boundary setting will help those parts to feel safe, because your responsible adult self is taking action internally and externally to protect that wounded inner child.

The metaphorical picket fence between you and another person is a way for you to remember that you can have boundaries by saying no when you feel that no. The picket fence also helps to remind you that just as you are on your own journey, the other person is on their journey, too. Respecting someone else's journey helps us to remember to stay on our side of the fence. It helps remind the codependent part of us that wants to fix, rescue, care-take, or control that it is not our job to run other people's lives or offer suggestions when we are not asked.

EXERCISE: THE PICKET FENCE

Picture yourself standing with someone you know. This could be someone you have a challenging time with or feel resentments toward. Now, in your mind's eye, see a picket fence between the two of you. Notice how you feel with the fence there. After you have had a few minutes to let your feelings arise, write down the answers to the following questions:

With the picket fence in place, does the relationship between you and this other person feel different from the usual?

_____

Do you feel safer with the fence in place?

_____

Do you feel safer with that person?

_____

Do you feel separate from them?

_____

Do you feel distant from them?

_____

Do you feel it may be easier to speak your truth and set a boundary with the fence there?

_____

With the picket fence in place, what is the boundary statement you want to make to the other person?

_____

Do you feel like you want to tear the fence down so you can be close to them?

_____

Are you tempted to make the fence larger and reinforced?

_____

Do you have a more balanced sense of self with the fence between you?

_____

Your reaction to this picket fence boundary can tell you more about your boundary status with this person and whether you need to adjust your boundaries with them. If the picket fence imagery helps you feel safer, this would be a good thing to remember as you are learning to set boundaries. If you want the fence to be higher or more solid, ask yourself what is happening emotionally. What reaction are you having that you feel you need a bigger wall instead of creating healthier boundary statements? We often feel the need to have a bigger wall when others talk over us or don't listen to us. This isn't about a wall, though, it is about a lack of respect within the relationship.

If the wounded part of you rejoices when you build a picket fence, then it is feeling safe and the picket fence is serving its purpose. If you want to tear the fence down so you can be closer to the other person, ask yourself if this a healthy relationship with healthy boundaries or if the picket fence feels too cold and unfeeling. Do you feel that the picket fence keeps you separate from this person or that it prevents you from loving and caring for them? These reactions are normal. Remember, you can still reach over the fence and give them a hug, so this boundary is not about not loving or caring for them.

If you feel emotionally safer on your side of the picket fence, think about what that tells you about your relationship with this person. Such a reaction means that you may need to evaluate and establish better boundaries with them. If you didn't have good boundaries with them before but the picket fence helps you to feel emotionally safer, you probably need to stand up for yourself more with that person, to say no, or to speak your mind in general.

Repeat the exercise for other people in your life to help you establish your current boundary status.

Self-Coaching

The following are examples of affirmations for supportive self-coaching to build self-esteem:

- I know this is hard, but I can do it.
- I am feeling stronger in myself every day, and I am worth it.
- I am trying my best, and I am proud of my efforts.
- Every day I am learning to set boundaries so I feel safe in my world.
- I am learning who I am and who I am not.
- I have a right to have my own feelings.
- I deserve to be treated with love and respect.
- I trust how I feel, and I express myself clearly to others.

These affirmations are just a few examples of how you can reassure yourself and affirm that everything you are doing is leading you to an expanded version of yourself. Write down some supportive self-coaching comments that you need to give yourself at this point. This may be difficult if you are not be used to using such language, but this kind and loving presence within will help to foster the gentle shifts that the HEAL process can create.

EXERCISE: SELF-COACHING

Write down the supportive messages you need to hear:

THE RESPONSIBLE ADULT SELF STEPS UP

At any given time, you have wounded parts that you are working on and parts that are healed and functional. The goal is to encourage your functional self, your responsible adult self, to step forward. This is the part that employs strong boundaries and is clear, authentic, and grounded. Having clarity between these parts of yourself will help you know the areas that need acknowledgment and healing.

Wounded and Functional Parts of the Self

Your wounded self may choose, feel, and express in some of the following ways. To the right of each word, write down when this feeling or expression happens. This may be a reaction to something internal or from something outside of you.

Your *wounded self* will choose, feel, and express in the following ways and when:

FEELING OR EXPRESSION

After each feeling write out what is usually happening for you to have this wounded reaction:

- Scared
- Victimized
- Blaming
- Resentful
- Uncertain
- Reactive
- Unaware

- Wary
- Confused
- Bewildered
- Wanting to avoid and hide

Your *functional self* will choose, feel, and express in the following ways and when:

FEELING OR EXPRESSION

After each feeling write out what is usually happening for you to have this functional reaction:
- Feeling solid
- Owning your life choices
- Practicing kindness toward self and others
- Being confident even when you don't know everything
- Being authentic
- Knowing who you are and who you are not
- Practicing self-control
- Being honest with yourself
- Accepting yourself and others
- Knowing when you are clear-headed and when you are distorting your truth

Your responsible adult self is like an internal kind, loving, and protective big brother or sister. It is the best of you, the part that you can count on to do the right thing and to show up.

The more you set boundaries, the more your wounded parts know and understand that your responsible adult self is going to be protective. The wounded parts will not let go of these wounded emotional response tools, no matter how destructive and dysfunctional they are, until your responsible adult self is able to consistently and confidently set internal and external boundaries. The wounded part is watching to see how, when, why, and where your responsible adult self addresses the situation whenever a wounding is triggered.

EXERCISE: HOW YOUR RESPONSIBLE ADULT SELF SHOWS UP

The following descriptions are various ways you can foster your responsible adult self to show up. Below each item, describe the type of situation and the emotional state you are in when it is easy for you to encourage your responsible adult self to show up. For example: *Trusting in myself and making the right choices is easy when I feel grounded, I've had enough sleep, and I am taking care of myself.* What do you need to encourage your responsible adult self to show up?

Maintain consistent grounded and functional responses to triggers.

_____

Have a clear sense of ownership on whether you are making a choice or not.

_____

Maintain a clear and open channel with your authentic self.

_____

Practice kind, loving, and respectful affirmations with yourself each day.

_____

Discern what feels right and what feels wrong.

_____

Have a clear and assertive way of addressing boundary violations.

_____

Know where, when, and how to look out for all parts of yourself in a functional way.

_____

Know how you want to show up for yourself.

_____

Your responsible adult self utilizes the functional response tools you developed as a child and as an adult. How has your responsible adult self shown up for you in the past? How does it show up now?

_____

The following is a list of functional response tools that you may have brought into adulthood. Under each one, write down the type of situation and the emotional state that you are in when it is easy for you to do the following:

Showing up for others

_____

_____

Asking for what you need

_____

_____

Loving yourself

_____

_____

Loving others

_____

_____

Practicing active gratitude with yourself and others

_____

_____

Listening to your needs

_____

_____

Hearing others, not just listening

_____

_____

Respecting others when they speak their truth, even when you don't understand it

_____

_____

Respecting the feelings of others, even when you don't understand them

_____

_____

Being vulnerable with others whom you trust

_____

_____

Sharing

_____

_____

Being kind

_____

_____

Offering to help others with no expectation of reciprocation

_____

_____

Thanking those around you

_____

_____

Practicing gratitude

_____

_____

Being proud of yourself, with humility

_____

_____

Having selfless pride in others

_____

_____

Finding courage when you are afraid

_____

_____

Practicing loving detachment in relationships when needed

_____

_____

Giving yourself permission to be vulnerable in relationships

_____

_____

Learning to let go of feelings of shame

_____

_____

Learning from others with humility

_____

_____

Trusting in yourself

_____

_____

By taking responsibility for yourself, you own your life choices, stop using your wounded emotional response tools, and start creating functional tools. In this exercise, you will determine the common things you need to encourage your responsible adult self to show up consistently.

EXERCISE: STANDING UP FOR YOURSELF

The following are common misconceptions you may have when you begin to set boundaries. What is your reaction to each of these statements? Why do you think you think or feel this way? Write your answers in the space below each item.

If I tell people how I feel, they won't like me.

_____

_____

_____

_____

I don't want other people to see me as angry or mean.

_____

_____

If I make a boundary statement, I have to live with it for life.

_____

_____

I am not a selfish person, and boundaries restrict my caring nature.

_____

_____

Standing up for yourself may not feel natural at first, and might even feel forced. This is normal, and getting used to exercising this muscle is going to take a while.

EXERCISE: STRENGTHEN YOUR "NO" MUSCLE

Let's begin to exercise your "no" muscle. Recall a situation when you said yes instead of honoring your no. Now suspend judgment and ask yourself why you made that choice. What were you avoiding, or what were you afraid of?

_____

_____

_____

_____

The reality is that our analytical minds know our games and will talk us into making choices and saying yes when we want to say no. Our minds play tricks with our emotional selves, our authentic selves. This is because we have had a lifetime of training our minds to override our authentic selves and our boundaries.

Recall again the situation when you said yes instead of no. Do you still think it was the best choice for you to have made to honor your authentic self? You may still say yes, and that's OK. The point is to ask yourself what your gut says the next time. Write down your thoughts here:

_____

_____

_____

_____

EXERCISE: OLD BOUNDARY PATTERNS

In this exercise you will list some life choices you have made that honored yourself, and some that did not. You will look at whether you honored your boundaries and stayed true to yourself, Works For Me, or went against your boundaries and made a choice to make someone else happy, Works For Them. Each day we make the best choices for ourselves based on our view of ourselves and the world. You made choices that satisfied others earlier in your life, when their happiness mattered more to you than your own. Your emotional wounding made the choices in the "Works for Them" column.

On the following page are two columns: "Works for Me" and "Works for Them." Recall a time when you said either yes or no to a situation or invitation. Think of the outcome, how you felt about it, and who you chose that yes or no answer for. Write a short description of the situation in the appropriate column. Do this for several situations.

WORKS FOR ME

WORKS FOR THEM

As a thought experiment, look at your "Works for Them" column and imagine what the outcomes would have been had you made different choices. Imagine what would have been different if you had honored your boundary system, and stood up for yourself and what you wanted. Would your life be different today?

Developing Your New Functional Tools

This exercise will help you to develop some new functional emotional response tools by understanding that you are in control of your mind, your mind is not in control of you. What instructions will you give your mind on how you want to experience yourself? You will answer two questions in the next exercise: Who do I want to be for myself? and How do I want to show up for others?

Before you begin the exercise, here are some examples of positive affirmations to encourage you to be *emotionally available to yourself.* You may use them as prompts for your answers:

- I am kind and gentle with myself.
- I find the motivation to go to the gym.
- I am proud that I eat well and nourish my body.
- I practice gratitude for all that is in my life.
- I honor my journey in recovery every day.
- I state my internal boundaries to myself clearly and lovingly.
- I am responsible with my choices when I smoke or drink.
- I respect my sense of self and know what is good for me and what isn't.
- I am learning to be emotionally vulnerable with myself.
- I can say no to someone, own it, and not feel guilty.
- I wake up each day and find the positive in life.
- I put a smile on my face to remind myself that I am loved.
- I am bringing humility into my life so that I may accept and love all parts of me.

Here are some examples of positive affirmations so you can be *emotionally available for others.* You may use them as prompts for your answers:

- I recognize when I need to be with others and when I need some alone time.
- I am truly present with my partner or spouse.
- I make good choices about who I surround myself with.
- I practice compassion for others.

- I honor my boundaries and choose others who do the same.
- I state my boundaries with others clearly and assertively.
- I am learning to be emotionally vulnerable to others and to not see it as a weakness.
- I feel good about who I am in my relationships.
- I respect the feelings of others, even when they don't make sense to me.
- I feel respected, loved, and trusted in my connections with others.
- My relationships feel reciprocal and nurturing.
- I practice humility in my relationships.
- I am opening my heart to those with whom I feel safe.

EXERCISE: WHO YOU WANT TO BE

Using the previous list of examples as a prompt, write down how you want to be for yourself in your day-to-day life. The language you use speaks to the part of you that is healing, so write in positive, present-tense language. How do you want to be the best you, for you?

WHO I WANT TO BE FOR MYSELF

Using the previous list of examples as a prompt, write down ideas of how you want to show up for others in your life. This is the best of you showing up for others.

HOW I WANT TO SHOW UP FOR OTHERS

The goals and ideals you wrote down in this exercise are not magic formulas that create immediate transformations or new situations in your life; they are ideals that you will begin to hold for yourself. Over time, they will help you to create new functional response tools.

Things You Would Like to Transform

You can manifest change in your life from the inside out through your intentions. This exercise will help you to see where you have power to change how you look at a situation and how you feel. Much of your healing work is simply about shifting your perspective.

EXERCISE: WHAT I WANT TO TRANSFORM

In the space below, write down some situations in your life that you would like to transform. Below each statement, brainstorm what you would change about the situation if you had a magic wand. As you review each item, ask yourself if there is an impulsive or wounded tool that stands in the way of your dreams. Is there something you believe or are doing that creates a roadblock for this transformation?

THINGS I WOULD LIKE TO TRANSFORM IN MY LIFE:

INTEGRATING
THE WOUNDED CHILD

Through each of the exercises in the workbook you have been working on creating a healing environment for your inner child. You are preparing yourself to intentionally live in an open, connected, and authentically free life. A good way to see how far you have come is to recognize where there are some gaps or situations in which you need to practice better boundaries. Having such gaps is completely normal, as you are learning new ways to connect to yourself and others.

Bridging the Gaps in Relationships

In your daily observation and discernment, you may notice that there are gaps in your life between having interactions that go well—when you are creating healthy, solid, strong connections—and when you go back to your old behaviors. This is a natural part of learning new skills; you are not going to be an expert right away. Gaps are the areas where you need to develop specific tools to use in a relationship or to consistently use the boundary tools you have developed.

Notice where you have safe connections, where a connection feels reciprocal, grounded, and nurturing. Now look at those areas where the connection feels uneven and you don't feel good about yourself or the connection. Notice where you are doing a good job at staying grounded and where there are some gaps in your functional response tools.

EXERCISE: CREATING INTENTIONS

Using the following intentions as a guide, create your own intentions that match the aspirations you have for your authentic life. After each intention, write out when it is easier and when it is harder for you to find the energy and motivation to give yourself the intention. For example, *I am kind and gentle with myself when I am patient and don't rush myself*, or, *I am kind and gentle with myself when I give myself gentle encouragement*. If you cannot add an extension to the intention, or if the intention is hard for you to own at this point, give yourself permission to pass on it for the moment. After each intention, write the conditions you need for it to happen.

I am kind and gentle with myself:

_____

I love myself:

_____

I trust myself:

_____

I respect myself:

_____

I find the motivation to move my body:

_____

I am proud that I am eating well and nourishing my body:

_____

I respect my sense of self, and I know what is good for me and what isn't:

_____

I can say no to someone, own it, and not feel guilty:

_____

Every day, in every way, I live my life to its fullest:

_____

My boundaries help me feel a sense of safety in my personal relationships:

_____

I make better choices about who I surround myself with on a daily basis:

_____

I feel good about who I am in my relationships with others:

_____

I feel respected, loved, and trusted by those in my life:

_____

My relationships nurture me and feel reciprocal:

_____

I bring others into my life who are emotionally healthy, and I create positive relationships:

_____

I am grateful that I continue to work on my relationship with myself:

_____

I am proud of all of my hard work and accomplishments:

Today I am wiser than I ever thought I could become:

PART II

Forming a Deeper Connection with Your Inner Child

Yesterday I was clever, so I wanted to change the world.
Today I am wise, so I am changing myself.
—Rumi

GOING DEEPER

You have completed some tremendous work in Part I, and now you have a better idea of your childhood wounding, how this shows up in your adult life, how to set boundaries, and ways to heal these recurring patterns. Part II will take you deeper into boundary setting, understanding codependency, self-nurturing, and much more, helping you to further integrate your inner child into your responsible adult self.

Some of these exercises are similar to those in Part I, but they go deeper and will give you insights into other dimensions of your inner self. The exercises are grouped together so you can jump to the area you want to explore the most to expand your awareness of self. You do not have to go in order.

Let's start with the following story of a smart woman who carried some of her lost inner child wounding into her adult life.

Story: The Overcompensating Inner Child

Angie told me that she had been deeply critical of herself for most of her life. Bright, funny, and engaging, she is a delight to work with, but her extreme self-criticism showed up every day, pointing out her flaws and all the things she could do better. She has a few close girlfriends, but she found it hard to develop emotional relationships with men.

As Angie worked through the HEAL process, she clearly identified a time in kindergarten when she was shamed. At five years old she loved going to kindergarten, working on assignments, and turning them in. She loved her teacher, who was loving and affirming, a perfect teacher for young children starting out in school. She always received good marks and smiley faces on her assignments, and she was proud of how well she was doing. One day, a substitute teacher filled in, and she gave the class an assignment. When the papers were graded, Angie's was returned with a low mark and a frowny face.

This low mark was devastating to five-year-old Angie. She had never received such a low score, and she wondered who this strange teacher was who took the place of her good, kind teacher. She was flush with shame and confusion.

As the school day ended and she was walking out with her friends, Angie crumpled up the assignment with the frowny face and threw it away. She was so embarrassed by this low mark, and felt so bad. She didn't want her mom to see it; the frowny face not only meant that she did a poor job on the assignment, it also meant that she herself was bad. At five years old, she internalized this message, and it broke her idea of herself that she was a good girl.

Decades later, Angie realized how this event was the start of lifelong self-criticizing language. Even though the event happened when she was such a young girl, her wounded inner child carried the shame into her adult life. Any time that she perceived someone thought she was doing something wrong or that she was bad, her lost inner child would impulsively come forward and reinforce her need to overcompensate, to push away men who might judge her, to overwork, and to try harder to be "greater than" herself.

Angie's wounded part also procrastinated on work assignments until the eleventh hour, then she would stay up all night getting the project done. She did not date because her wounded child self didn't feel worthy to meet someone else. She would think, *If only others knew how bad and damaged I am.*

When Angie wrote her healing letters, she began to remember more examples from her childhood that contributed to her narrative. She began to piece together how her idea of herself developed, and she realized that it was "just so stupid that I let it take over my life."

As she healed and practiced boundary setting, she got a handle on this out-of-control five-year-old, who kept making reactionary and impulsive decisions in her adult life. She was able to calm this part down and begin to integrate her lost inner child with her responsible adult self.

Angie's main emotional themes were of overcompensating so others didn't see her flaws, fearing rejection, and having too much or too little ego—an internal seesaw.

Using the HEAL process, you can go back in time and hold and comfort your younger self. Life is hard enough that you don't need to keep beating up on yourself.

In all of the stories you read in the book, each person was trying to do their best with the knowledge they had at the time. I believe this is true for all of us. No one wakes up in the morning and thinks, *How can I screw up my life today? Oh, I know! I will attach this irrational belief to myself and then believe it every day until it really screws me up!*

I believe that we all determine the best things we can do each day that will help us along our path. We use all of our accumulated knowledge to create a plan, and we do our best with that plan. We can also look back and ask ourselves why we made certain choices, but each day, that idea or plan sounded good to us. It was the best decision at the time.

Remember to be gentle with yourself as you work through these exercises. If you get into cycles of regret or shame, just calmly tell yourself, *I did my best with what I knew at the time. Today I would make a different choice.*

EXERCISE: YOUR IMPRESSIONS

Are there any parts of Angie's story that sound like aspects of your story? Write down your impressions. This may help you with later assignments in the workbook.

_____

_____

_____

EXERCISE: A QUICK SNAPSHOT

Without giving it a lot of thought, write down a few feeling words below to describe how you are feeling right now. Some feeling words are happy, pensive, neutral, joyful, and wondering. (See table 1 in the introduction for more feeling words.)

Right now I feel:

_____

Right now my inner child feels:

_____

Daily Connection with Your Inner Child

Your lost inner child is looking for connection from you each day. Get used to forming this connection with this part of you, because the more you acknowledge it, the less hard it has to work to get your attention.

EXERCISE: CONNECT WITH YOUR INNER CHILD

To practice this connection, close your eyes, be still for a minute or so, and ask your inner child what it needs right now. Based on how your inner child feels, write down what it needs right now (e.g., love, affirmation, validation):

_____

_____

_____

EXERCISE: GIVE YOUR INNER CHILD A VOICE

In the space below, write down one or two words to describe how your inner child feels most days (see table 1 for feeling words):

Most days the wounded or hurt part of me feels:

_____

Describe how this part feels and shows up in your life today by filling in the blanks:
I feel:

_____

when:

_____

Write down how long you have felt this way (in days or years):

I have felt this way for:_____

What behavior does your inner child use to demonstrate the feeling? For example, "When my inner child feels lonely, I isolate and withdraw." Write down how this feeling shows up in your life most days:

When I feel:

_____

I usually show it in these ways:

_____

_____

This behavior helps my inner child by (e.g., *It helps my inner child feel safe*, or *It just feels familiar*):

_____

_____

When I behave this way, my inner child feels:

_____

_____

You have identified your inner child's feeling and associated behaviors. Can you determine the root of this acting out, what is under the feelings? For example, *When I say I feel lonely, what I'm really trying to say is that I want, wish, desire, hope that . . .*

Write down what your inner child is trying to communicate through this behavior:

_____

_____

_____

Once you know what your inner child is trying to communicate to you, ask what it needs to address this feeling as an alternative to acting out, such as reassurance, comforting, or validation. Write down your answers below.

My inner child needs:

_____

If I can give this to myself, then I won't need to act out.

Sometime it is hard to give my inner child what it needs because:

_____

I know I need to give this to that part of myself, but I hold back because:

_____

This holding back is an old pattern connected to:

_____

If I were to be good to myself, I would feel:

_____

A Deeper Connection with Your Lost Inner Child

You are now connecting to some core feelings with your inner child, and are getting to know what that part of you is trying to tell you. You are also learning why it may be hard to give to yourself that which you need to heal.

Sometimes being gentle and loving with yourself is hard if you never received that as a child. It can be hard to find kind words to express to yourself. At the same time, you may find that your adult self is just as lost and wounded as your inner child. This mirroring can shut down the process of letter writing and other exercises. You may feel that you don't have the skills available to attend to the wounded part, but that is not entirely the case.

You may not know what to say or how to interact with your wounded inner child. You may think that you don't have many functional response tools, and are struggling. However, you use more functional adult tools to interact with the world than you realize. For instance, you may have mentored, reassured, or given guidance to young people. In those cases, the best part of you stepped up and attended to their feelings. You were gentle, kind, and reassuring, and you watched as they responded to you, and you saw how they felt safer and more at ease. Imagine right now how you would comfort a young child who feels lonely, unworthy, sad, confused, and upset. You would probably say something to reassure them and help them feel better.

EXERCISE: YOUR WOUNDED CHILD PERSPECTIVE

This exercise will help you connect to how your younger wounded part feels and to find words of comfort to give to yourself. If necessary, review the Needs Inventory in table 2 in the introduction to identify what you needed as a child but didn't get.

Complete the following sentences:

When I was younger, most of the time I felt:

_____

I wish that someone in my young life would have:

_____

When I did tell someone how I felt, they would often:

_____

Deep down, I often felt that:

_____

I didn't always tell people how I felt, but I would:

_____

I wanted them to know I was hurting when I:

_____

The three things I would love to have heard as a child are:

_____

When people try to comfort or reassure me, I find their gestures hard to believe because:

_____

As much as I want to accept positive or good feelings, I can't because:

_____

When I wonder how other people are doing so well, I feel:

_____

My inner child feels this way about the healing work that I am doing:

_____

My inner child knows that what happened when I was a child isn't happening now, but this part still feels:

_____

Now look at this from your adult perspective.
I think my inner child needs to hear:

_____

but the adult part of me feels:

_____

When I try to give my inner child what it needs, I feel:

_____

When I watch parents be kind to their own children, I learn:

_____

I can be kind to my own children as well as others, but I can't give this kindness to my inner child because:

_____

I can't be kind and gentle with my inner child because most days I feel:

_____

I am scared that if I start communicating with my inner child, this wounded part will:

_____

The biggest emotion I think my inner child carries is:

_____

Because of this emotion, my first instinct is to:

_____

I want to hug my inner child, but I resist this because:

_____

For me to be able to attend to my inner child, I first need to:

_____

Sometimes I get in my own way by:

_____

Today I give myself permission to be kind and loving to my inner child. To succeed, I need to tell myself:

_____

I know it may take a while to form a connection with my inner child. This makes me feel:

_____

When I struggle to find the words to say to my inner child, I need to remember:

_____

My inner child probably needs to hear the same three things that I needed to hear as a child. They are:

_____

If I were to say these three things to my inner child, that part would feel:

_____

I feel grateful that I am:

_____

My inner child is feeling better, so my adult self is feeling:

_____

Each day that I do this work for myself, I feel:

_____

I want to give my wounded parts some reassurance, but I can't because:

_____

When I try to be positive and comforting with myself, I feel:

_____

No one ever gave me what I needed, so I don't know how to:

_____

When I use reassuring words with myself, I feel like I am:

_____

The three people in my life who I consider positive, functional adult role models are:

_____

I consider them role models because they have these attributes:

_____

I try to model my behavior after them, but I sometimes feel:

_____

I know my wounded parts need to hear from me, but I:

_____

I sometimes resist the urge to connect to my younger self because:

_____

I promise to myself and my inner child that each day I will:

_____

Remember to be gentle with yourself as you learn how to communicate with your inner child, and how and when your responsible adult self steps forward. You are a work in progress. You know more than you think you do, and you have already healed more than you know.

EMOTIONAL RESPONSE TOOLS

As adults, we respond to situations based on our collective experiences from birth. We develop these responses based on behaviors that were modeled by the adults in our lives or by developing responses on our own. We carry these emotional response tools with us wherever we go. Some of these tools help us to create better relationships, and some we use damage or destroy relationships.

There are two types of emotional response tools, functional responses and impulsive reactions (also referred to as wounded emotional response tools), and they are all jumbled together in our emotional response toolbox. Sometimes using an impulsive reaction tool, such as yelling or blaming, is easier because when we are deeply upset, it is easier and quicker to grab the tool of lashing out in anger rather than maturely and responsibly talking about what is happening. At other times, finding functional response tools, such as being respectful and reasonable, is easy if we take our time. We choose this type of tool when we can take a deep breath and become grounded and clear, because we have learned that when we use a wounded impulsive reaction, we don't always get a good outcome.

Wounded Emotional Response Tools

We all have our own typical knee-jerk responses to certain situations when we are triggered. These are the impulsive response tools that our lost inner child uses to protect us from harm. They don't help us create healthy relationships with others, yet we hold on to them because they are what we know.

EXERCISE: YOUR WOUNDED EMOTIONAL RESPONSE TOOLS

By now you know the top three to five wounded response tools that you typically grab when you are triggered. If you need to refresh your memory, review your answers in "Exercise: Your Impulsive Response Tools" in chapter 1.

As you review these tools, remember why you started using them. Perhaps you saw a family member have this response, so you started doing it. Or maybe it just felt right to you. Recall when you started using each tool. Were you a child, in your teens, or in early adulthood?

Complete the following sentences:

My top three to five wounded tools are:

_____

_____

_____

_____

_____

I still grab each tool because:

_____

_____

_____

I hold on to each one because:

_____

_____

_____

_____

When I use each of these wounded tools, I feel:

_____

_____

_____

Today my wounded response tools serve me by:

_____

_____

_____

I use these wounded tools most often in response to these people and situations:

_____

_____

_____

If I were to let go of my wounded responses, I would feel:

_____

If others saw me respond differently than I normally do, they might think:

_____

I want to give up these wounded response tools, but I hold on to them tightly because:

_____

When I respond with a wounded tool, I usually get this result:

_____

Overall, the wounded response tools I still use cause this in my life:

_____

As you wrote out your answers, what did you learn about your wounded response tools?

_____

Do they still serve you?

_____

Functional Emotional Response Tools

The functional emotional response tools of showing empathy, and being kind and generous toward yourself and others, are easy to use when you are grounded, calm, and have a clear perspective. Grabbing a functional response tool when you are triggered or agitated is harder. Our natural inclination is to respond impulsively and to defend ourselves with what we know has worked in the past, which is usually a wounded tool. You have functional emotional response tools in your toolbox, but you may not be clear about what they are.

EXERCISE: YOUR FUNCTIONAL EMOTIONAL RESPONSE TOOLS

By now you may know your top three to five functional emotional response tools. To refresh your memory, review your answers to "Exercise: Your Functional Response Tools" in chapter 2.

As you review these tools, remember why you started using them. Perhaps you saw a family member have this response, so you started doing it. Or maybe it just felt right to you. Recall when you started using each tool. Were you a child, in your teens, or in early adulthood?

Write down the top three to five functional emotional response tools you use in most situations. Next to each tool, write down the emotional state you need to be in to grab it:

_____

_____

_____

Complete the following sentences:

When I use a functional response tool I feel:

_____

These functional response tools allow me to have a better life by:

_____

_____

I use these functional tools most often in response to these people and situations:

_____

_____

_____

If I were to respond with functional tools all the time, I would feel:

_____

If others saw me respond differently than I normally do, they might think:

_____

I would like to use these functional tools more often, but:

_____

Looking over my life, it has been easier to use a functional response tool when:

_____

I used to use these functional response tools:

_____

but I no longer use them because:

_____

I no longer use functional tools with these people or in these specific situations:

_____

because:

_____

The functional response tools that I want to continue to develop and use are:

_____

_____

_____

As you go about your day, notice when you feel balanced and grounded. These times are when you are probably using tools from your functional toolbox.

TRIGGERS

In Part I you worked on identifying some of your triggers. In this section, you will go a little deeper to discover what triggers you and how you can acknowledge and heal this wounding.

What Triggers You

We all get irritated, frustrated, or triggered from a situation or type of person we encounter. Some people don't like to be disrespected, for example, and others don't like to be ignored. The following exercise will help you go deeper in exploring your triggers.

EXERCISE: WHAT TRIGGERS YOU

In the blanks below, write down the situations and the types of people that trigger you. You may have multiple triggers, which is normal. Write them down.

I feel:

_____

when someone does this to me:

_____

I feel:

_____

when this happens in a situation:

_____

Look over you answers, and consider for a moment that the trigger within you is not so much about the other person as it represents an unhealed part of you. Resist the urge to blame the other person or a situation, and look at what you need to do to heal the wounding inside that gets triggered. Realizing this now, what is the wounding you would like to heal next?

_____

EXERCISE: GENTLE DETACHMENT FROM TRIGGERS

Think back over the last week and your interactions with others and situations. Recall an experience or situation that didn't work out well and that has stayed with you. When you think of this situation, what are some feelings that come up?

_____

Was your inner child triggered?

_____

If your inner child was triggered, what behavior did it use as a response?

_____

Go deeper into your connections with your inner child by completing the following statements: My inner child shows up when I am:

_____

I am learning what my inner child sounds and feels like, but knowing for certain is hard because:

_____

My inner child gets triggered when I am with:

_____

When I hear:_____
my inner child feels:

_____

Recently my inner child was feeling: _____
about this situation or person:

_____

I connect with and calm my inner child when I tell myself:

_____

I am now able to observe how I react to a situation because I am:

_____

I am learning to not beat up on myself when things go wrong because I now realize:

_____

I know that my inner child is showing up when:

_____

My inner child gets scared, quiet, or loud when I am with these people:

_____

My inner child gets scared, quiet, or loud when I am in this situation:

_____

My inner child doesn't want to give up its defenses because:

_____

It is sometimes hard for me to be kind to my inner child because:

_____

I am always cleaning up after my inner child makes an impulsive decision; as a result, I feel:

_____

EXERCISE: YOUR PERSONAL THEME

We all carry a "theme" about who we are. For example, some people are rescuers, some people are always looking to restore justice, some people get hung up on others' hypocrisy, and some people do not tolerate being disrespected. What are some of the themes you see in yourself? What behaviors do you dislike, whether directed toward you or someone else?

My personal life theme is:

_____

I dislike these behaviors in others:

_____

When you consider your theme, does it serve you? Or do you use it to justify controlling others so you feel safer? Or do you hide behind the theme so you don't have to deal with your real feelings or resolve any wounding inside of yourself? Write your thoughts:

_____

_____

HEALING LETTERS REDUX

In Part I you practiced writing healing letters to and from your younger self. You may have had a hard time writing these letters, so I have included an alternative approach in this chapter.

Healing Letters Mad Libs™ Style

Mad Libs[1] is a fill-in-the-blank form of writing that can make the idea of healing letter writing easier for you. Try the following templates for a different take on your healing letters.

EXERCISE: HEALING LETTERS MAD LIBS STYLE

Try creating a letter from your younger self by filling in the blanks in the following template. Begin by connecting to and feeling what was happening during your age of wounding. Remember, you know all of this; you lived it. (Hint: Don't overthink your answers; just connect with your wounded part, and let it flow.) Write in the present tense, as your lost inner child believes the trauma is still happening and is stuck.

---

1 Mad Libs is a registered trademark of Penguin Random House, LLC.

Dear adult me,

I feel really _____ right now. The people in my life, especially

_____, have been _____ lately. I'm _____

years old, and I feel _____ and _____ most of the

time. I try to _____ or tell others what is going on with me, but I feel

_____, and they often just _____. When I

can't find the right words, I act out by _____. Sometimes

I do this _____ and _____. Other times I do

this _____. I feel _____ even when I

feel _____, but I just try to keep _____. I need to

tell others that I'm _____. No one gives me _____,

which is what I really need. When things like this _____ happen

at home or school, I feel _____. But no one else seems to

_____. Right now I feel _____.

From, younger me

Now try one from your adult self in response to your younger self's letter. Write in present tense, and be sure to address all of the emotional pain your younger part has expressed feeling.

Dear younger me,

I know that you feel _____ most of the time and that this doesn't

always feel _____. I want you to know that I hear you say that you

feel _____ and _____. I want you to know that you are not

_____. When things like _____ happen at _____

[place/time] or _____, I know that you feel _____ . This is all

very _____, and I know that sometimes you want to _____.

I want you to know that I see your _____, and that I'm here for you. I'm not

going anywhere, and we are going to get through this _____. I also want you

to know that I'm learning ways to _____. I'm also using these

boundaries _____ to make sure that all parts of us are safe.

I know that you sometimes act out by _____ when you feel _____,

and that this makes you feel better and a little in control for a short time. But I'm learning

new and healthier ways of feeling safe and in control. I can help all parts of us to feel safe and

protected in our relationships by using these boundaries. I am never far away, and I'm always

_____ for you. Together we will become stronger, and one day you will not

feel so _____. One day you will be integrated with me as an adult, and it will

feel _____. I want you to know and feel that I _____ you and will be there

for _____ .

Love, adult me

HEALING LETTERS REVIEW

Take a moment to look over the letters you wrote. You may have found it easier than you thought, or you may not have realized you were feeling all of those emotions. Many people are surprised by all of the feelings and memories that come flooding out of them.

These fill-in-the-blank letters are meant as a guide to help you get a feel for the back-and-forth style of letter writing. Use the first template to create another free-form, stream-of-consciousness letter from your younger self to your adult self. Your younger wounded parts have a lot of information to share with you. See if you can be kind and gentle with your younger self. After all, this part has worked hard to keep you safe for all these years. All of this emotion has been pent up for a long time and needs to be expressed. This is the perfect time to get it all out. Once you do, you probably will feel lighter and better.

CODEPENDENCY

Many people have no idea what the word *codependency* means. At its core, codependency is when a person cares for, loves, and respects someone else more than they do themselves. It is an adaptive emotional response to something we want to fix. Codependent skills are, essentially, wounded response tools. This idea of caring for or loving someone more than oneself may sound altruistic, and at times it is, but the systematic denial of self-care and self-love is what makes codependent behaviors so intrinsically damaging.

When children are old enough to see, sense, and feel their world, and to consciously integrate with their family, they see the world with innocence and curiosity through their own personality and emotional framework. Children whose families are chaotic and dysfunctional, which most are to some degree, adapt their personality to their family environment. Adapted children reshape themselves to fit into the dysfunctional family dynamic because that is what they believe they need to do to emotionally survive the chaotic environment. They look at the situation and realize that they have to make it work. They want to be loved, they want to emotionally survive in their family, and they want everyone to be happy.

Codependency and Relationships

Chronic stress within the family can create a developmental trauma, what is known as an attachment trauma, in the child, which may be a risk factor for any number of mental, emotional, and physical illnesses later in life. Children are extremely resilient and responsive, and will learn how to adapt and align with the energy of their family system. They independently figure out their reactions to stressful events by using a system of trial and error, trying to get the setting right for the family dance. They use adaptation, intuition, resilience, intelligence, and the emotions of love and fear to have a sense of belonging and connection. Over time, they use this accumulated knowledge to make their role within the family work. Subconsciously, children attempt to make the dysfunctional functional.

Children also observe their parents' adaptive skills. By carefully observing how their mother acts out, for example, the child learns an unhealthy way of expressing emotion. The impressionable child may learn how to rage and not know or understand healthy ways to express anger. Similarly, the child may observe, for example, how their father chooses to be passive, doesn't set boundaries, and doesn't claim his personal power. The child is learning to doubt natural feelings and to believe that words do not have value. Everyone in this family dynamic is doing their best, but they are each acting out their own unresolved emotions in a subconscious, codependent way.

JUDGING CODEPENDENT BEHAVIORS

When we judge someone for learning codependent behavior as a child and claim that it is bad, we imply that the child was bad for developing these skills. Such judgment can cause a lot of shame in someone who, as a child, was responding the best they could at the time. Becoming a people pleaser—working extra hard to help Dad because they could see Dad was hurting, for example—felt right to this young child. Or becoming withdrawn and extra quiet when Mom was yelling felt right to do. This child was figuring out a complex collection of wounded tools to use when needed to survive. They would carry these tools into their adult life, and play out the same scenarios within adult relationships, often using the same wounded tools.

Viewing codependent behaviors that were developed in childhood as coping skills reframes the behaviors and removes the shame of having innocently learned these intuitive and instinctual survival behaviors. Seeing codependent behaviors as skills allows us to look at them differently so we can create a new, positive narrative. I believe that when we take this more positive approach, we give both the adult self and the child self a sense of agency so that we can make choices about these adaptive behaviors and feelings.

CODEPENDENCY AS AN ADULT

When you use codependent behaviors, you involve others in your unresolved issues, creating a never-ending cycle. Subconsciously, you are inviting them to reenact your childhood wounding, with no one any the wiser. When you give your power away by making others better and greater, and yourself smaller, your narrative about yourself can morph into something very different from what you imagine or even want.

Instead of reenacting this drama and being smothered by shame, you can learn how to give yourself self-love and self-care, which is the antidote to codependency. You cannot get to healing by berating yourself into doing better. You get to a place of healing by giving yourself kindness, love, compassion, caring, and understanding. Caring for and loving yourself, and setting boundaries, are what heals codependent patterns.

If you have codependent behaviors, be kind to your lost inner child, who worked hard at a young age to learn those adaptive skills. Your inner child needs to hear and feel your compassion. This part needs to know that you respect the sense of agency in creating wounded tools to help you to make it through a dysfunctional family and out the other side.

Celebrate the adaptive skills you developed at an early age to survive dysfunctional environments. Celebrate the fact that you figured out on your own how to navigate an emotionally upsetting environment. Look at how you made an intolerable situation work by figuring out what you needed to do. Now, this is not a celebration of codependency; it is a celebration of your having developed the skills to survive a dysfunctional environment. It is about celebrating the fact that you are working toward healing your codependent patterns so that you can embrace thriving. The codependent patterns served you well then, but they are probably not serving you well today.

The following is a story about a child who was trying his best to make sense of a very difficult family dynamic by using his wounded response tools.

Story: The Child Who Thought He Wasn't Worth Loving

Jasper came to see me because he wanted to stop lying to his wife. He didn't understand why he kept telling her "stupid" white lies. He had tried all sorts of tricks, which I call *mechanical interventions*: he used a rubber band to snap his wrist when he told a lie, put up inspirational reminders, and tried other things, but nothing worked. His wife, Alicia, was near her breaking point after years of his lying to her. He was at his wits' end, too. He didn't want to lose his family and disappoint his boys. I guided him through the HEAL process, including creating his timeline.

A big emotional standout on Jasper's timeline was when he was six years old; his mom and dad divorced, and his dad moved out. Afterward, Jasper had minimal contact with his dad. His mom remarried, and his stepfather took his dad's place. From this time on, Jasper felt aimless, and acted out at home and school. The family moved almost every year, so he was always changing schools and trying to make new friends.

Jasper was learning how to fit in, "read" people, and adapt to new situations. He was learning the codependent skills of changing himself into whatever he thought his new friends wanted him to be, and to only say what he thought they wanted to hear, so that he would be liked and accepted. In other words, he was learning to lie and avoid. Underneath all of this, he felt unworthy, scared, and lonely.

At twelve years old, Jasper started smoking, drinking, hanging out with the wrong crowd, and stealing small items from stores. Even though he was trying to act tough and fit in, inside he was frightened and felt alone.

He would cry into his pillow at night, wanting to stop the behaviors and get out of the cycles, but he didn't know how. Eventually, his mom had enough of his acting out, and sent him to live with his dad at the beginning of high school. By this point, many of his wounded response tools were established. His dad, meanwhile, had healed parts of himself, and now he wanted to have a connection with his teenage son. But like most teens, Jasper wanted more independence and to not have much to do with his dad.

When Jasper reviewed his timeline, he identified his age of wounding as six years old, when his parents divorced. He remembered thinking that if he was so easy to abandon, then he must not be worth loving. This early narrative began to make an impression on all parts of his sense of self and how he looked at life. He took on this misperception of himself because of his parents' choices, how they handled the divorce, and the fact that they did not establish a context to help him understand emotionally what was happening. As a six-year-old child, Jasper had had no way to put his complex feelings into words, but as an adult, he easily identified this sense of abandonment and being unworthy of love.

The inner child carries the wounded codependent skills into adulthood because that is what the inner child knows to do. Using the HEAL process, Jasper went on to set stronger boundaries for himself and with his wife. He learned how to express his feelings instead of avoiding them, even if others didn't like what he was saying. He learned to use his functional tools to create a safe place for his lost inner child to integrate with his adult self.

Now that he feels stronger, today Jasper is reevaluating his life choices. He no longer reacts to life; he thinks about what he wants to do to create his life. He no longer lies or avoids confrontations. He doesn't like confrontations, but today he knows that people aren't going to leave him just because he speaks his truth. By helping his inner child heal, all parts of him now feel stronger, and he has a great deal of clarity.

As you work through this section, think about your age of wounding and the wounded tools you have carried into adulthood. Think back to how you adapted to emotionally survive in your childhood family. Know that you did your best with what you knew, and know that today you can make a choice of how you want to heal and transform your outdated wounded reactions.

EXERCISE: CODEPENDENT BEHAVIORS ASSESSMENT

The following is a partial list of the ways codependency manifests. Circle those that you think, use, or do:

- Caretake others
- Fix things for others
- Rescue others
- Distract yourself with other people's problems so you don't have to look at your own
- Think others are better than you
- Say things to yourself that keep you down
- Give your power away to someone else
- Make up stories about someone else because you feel nervous or insecure
- Let someone else determine your reality
- Have no boundaries as a way to escape responsibility
- Make no choices so others can't say you made a "wrong" choice
- Behave like a victim in the hope that someone will rescue you
- Behave like a victim for attention
- Test others to see if they care
- Control others or an outcome so you feel safe
- Stay in toxic relationships because you are afraid of change
- Avoid setting any boundaries because you don't want others to be mad at you
- Read the moods of others so that you can anticipate their needs, foregoing your own needs
- Make things comfortable for someone else while ignoring your own needs
- Try to be perfect so others don't see what you don't like about yourself
- Smile and say things are "fine" to keep others at arm's length
- Avoid speaking your truth when asked a direct question
- Ignore what you want to do, and give in to someone else's wants

Do you see a crossover between these codependent behaviors and your wounded response tools? Write down the connections between the two that you can identify within yourself:

_____

_____

Complete the following sentences about the codependent behaviors you identified:

I believe I still react this way because:

_____

I still use these adaptive skills today because:

_____

The trends I see in my behavior are:

_____

I react with codependent behaviors to this type of person or situation:

_____

When I was a child, I learned or my parents instilled in me these distorted realities:

_____

I see life through a distorted lens of wounding by these behaviors:

_____

Now think about how you want to heal and transform each of the codependent traits that you identified.

I want to heal and transform these reactions:

_____

_____

by doing these things:

_____

_____

Going forward, make a point to observe yourself in your relationships. See where you give your power away and put others' wants and needs above your own. Observe how you use the codependent skills you learned as a child, and how you play them out in your adult relationships. As you do the exercises in this workbook, you are learning how to acknowledge your feelings and how to set functional healthy boundaries. By using these new functional tools, you are moving on from your codependent responses toward developing healthier relationships.

CIRCLE OF CONNECTION

We all have people who are close to us, who are in our inner circle. We also have people who are on the edge or outside of our circle. We instinctively connect deeply with some, while others are acquaintances, people we keep at arm's length. Our natural connections with these groups of people, and our varying degrees of closeness, give us a sense of belonging, community, and connection.

Your Circle of Connection

Some people stay in our inner circle for a lifetime, and others just visit. This natural flow of connection and disconnection is what creates a rich life experience. We are not static beings, we are moving, changing, growing, and evolving all of the time.

Sometimes our wounding causes us to choose certain people to bring into our inner circle because the wounding feels that they belong there. As we heal, we begin to realize that some of these people don't treat us respectfully, or we have emotionally outgrown them. We reevaluate whether to have them in our inner circle.

The following exercise will allow you to evaluate who is in and who is out of your circle of connection, and to see if you need to make some adjustments in order to align your connections with who you are today.

EXERCISE: YOUR CIRCLE OF CONNECTION

For this exercise, you will create a circle of friends and family so that you can see exactly who you have in your life. You will be able to see the connections you have that are fulfilling and satisfying, and the connections that are toxic or codependent. Read through the exercise first, then fill out the circle in figure 3.

Write your name in the middle of the circle. Inside the circle, write the names of friends or family whom you feel are healthy, reciprocal, respectful, good for you, and who you feel good around.

Outside of the circle, write the names of the people in your life who are toxic, disrespectful, or needy; who bring you down or don't listen to you; and who you don't feel close to or can't wait to get away from. Include people whom you feel you have to adapt or change for so that they will like or love you. These are people with whom you have a codependent relationship.

You may know some people who are on the edge of the circle. Sometimes these people are emotionally stable and you have fun with them, but other times they are just a lot of work. You may be married to them, in partnership with them, work with or for them, or are part of the family. In other words, for the time being you feel stuck with them, but you wouldn't choose them. Write their names on the edge of the circle.

FIGURE 3. YOUR CIRCLE OF CONNECTION

To recap: inside of the circle are people with whom you can be your authentic self and feel connected and safe. Outside the circle are people who you change yourself for, who are toxic and who you don't feel emotionally safe with. On the edge of the circle are people who are sometimes emotionally healthy for you and sometimes not.

Look at your circle and note who is inside the circle and who is out. Notice your reaction to where you placed the people in your life. You may be shocked to realize the toxic or unfulfilling connections you have. Just observe your internal reaction to this exercise.

Sometimes people want to immediately get rid of all the toxic relationships. However, this exercise is not about firing any of your family, partners, friends, or coworkers; it is about asking yourself why you keep the relationships that are not serving you. Ask yourself why you keep putting up with situations that you know are not good for you, and why you let others treat you this way. The answer always comes back to unresolved emotions and unresolved and unhealed wounding that is reflected in our relationships.

If many of the names you wrote down are on the edge or outside of your circle, you may be doing what I did before I was healed. Recall from chapter 3 in *HEALing Your Lost Inner Child* that I held on to many friendships that were not healthy for me, either out of a sense of loyalty or because I didn't want to hurt those people. As I got healthier emotionally, I realized that they were not good for me, because they put me down or kept me down. I was reenacting my old wounding with them, and I didn't know it. I thought I was OK and doing well, but the truth was that I was giving my power to them all of the time.

Many people live in illusions created by their emotional wounding. They don't realize that their partners or friends are not emotionally well. This is especially true for codependents, as they keep bending themselves into pretzel shapes to fit into someone else's reality. They lose sight of themselves and what they want and need. This is how codependent people attract toxic friends and relationships.

EXERCISE: FRIENDS AND FAMILY CIRCLE REVIEW

Look over your circle again. To look deeper, complete the following sentences:
When I look at the people inside my circle I feel:

_____

When I look at the people outside of my circle I feel:

_____

The people who are inside my circle are for the most part (list their qualities):

_____

_____

The people who are outside my circle are for the most part (list their qualities):

_____

The people who I feel closest to and can be myself with are:

_____

I feel safe with those inside my circle because:

_____

I am not able to be myself with those outside my circle because:

_____

I have _tried_ to mend my relationships with some people outside my circle because:

_____

I have _not tried_ to mend my relationships with some people outside my circle because:

_____

I don't want to repair the relationship with:

_____

because:

_____

I don't understand why I maintain a connection with:

_____

I keep relationships going with those whom I consider toxic because:

_____

I can't give up my codependent behaviors with these people because:

_____

I maintain the connection with these people because they know a lot about me:

_____

The next statements will take you deeper into specific relationships.
I wish I hadn't shared my private information with:

_____

because:

_____

This person shared my private information without my consent:

_____

and I now feel:

_____

I thought that by sharing my personal information with them, I would create a stronger bond, but instead it just created:

_____

The trends or patterns I see in this relationship are:

_____

I realize that I was trying to keep a connection with this person, but it is not a healthy relationship. Before I make a decision about what to do, I will look within and understand the following better:

_____

_____

EXERCISE: HOW YOU CHANGE YOURSELF FOR OTHERS

In this exercise, you will explore how you change yourself for others. Think of a person in your outer circle with whom you have a toxic relationship. Think about what you know about that person and how you make yourself smaller and less-than when you are around them. Complete the following statements about that person.

I am usually myself except when I am around: _____
When I am around this person, I often:

_____

I hold back speaking my truth with this person because:

_____

My guess is that I change myself when I am around this person because:

_____

I have tried to just be myself around this person, but:

_____

Consider the broader group of people outside your circle, then complete the following statements: When I am around other people who are:

_____

I will often:

_____

I change or adapt myself when I am with others because:

_____

When I change myself for someone else, afterward I feel:

_____

Others have told me that I change or act differently when:

_____

It is hard for me to take a compliment from others because:

_____

For reasons I don't understand, I keep bringing this type of person into my life:

_____

By now you see that unresolved emotional issues show up in your adult life and those of many of your partners, friends, and coworkers. Once you work on your own wounding and are honest with yourself, you begin to see similar patterns in others: the boss who throws tantrums or pouts, the partner who shuts down or becomes passive-aggressive, the friend who is highly insecure and always needs reassurance. These are all examples of how emotional wounding can show up in others.

Think about the emotional response tools the people in your life use. Notice how you have adapted yourself to their wounded child, how you have learned how to accommodate their hurt, how you turn a blind eye to their toxicity or dysfunction. To develop a functional tool for dealing with these people, see if you can be present and available for their wounded part without changing yourself. You are not being uncaring; you are respecting yourself first, and acknowledging how you have been changing yourself to maintain this relationship.

You now have the advantage of seeing these wounds more clearly, but you can't change or control anyone else. So, what can you do? This is where compassion and boundary setting come forth. It is easier to have compassion or empathy for someone else if you have healed your own emotional wounding. Your compassionate side is able to come forth. You can have empathy for someone else and observe where they are.

You can extend this kindness as you watch them rage, withdraw, isolate, attack, or self-harm. This does not mean that you let yourself be abused or injured. You still need to protect yourself and set boundaries as needed. Say no when you need to. Let your feelings be known.

Be kind to the shadow of your former self. —Rev. Don Burt

EXERCISE: TOXIC PEOPLE IN YOUR LIFE

Complete the following statements about the toxic people in your life, those on the outside of your circle.

My guess is that I keep finding the same type of toxic person because:

_____

I seem to date or have toxic friends, and because of this I feel:

_____

I have tried to change the pattern of allowing toxic people into my life, but I:

_____

Sometimes I keep toxic people in my circle because it is easier than:

_____

I keep letting toxic people say mean things to me or not treat me well because:

_____

I am OK with keeping some of my friends who I know are bad for me because I:

_____

Those around me tell me I keep repeating toxic patterns, and this makes me feel:

_____

Sometimes I wish I hadn't met this person: _____
because:

_____

The wisdom I have today about my toxic relationships is:

_____

I want to forgive myself for making bad relationship choices, but:

_____

This idea of myself holds me back from moving on:

_____

I would feel deserving of a better life if I would have:

_____

The illusion of being undeserving comes from:

_____

Today I am willing (within myself) to symbolically give back the illusion of being undeserving to:

_____

I am also willing to give up the idea of unworthiness because:

_____

Today I give up the idea of being less-than because:

_____

Three things that I think about myself that no longer serve me are:

_____

_____

Giving up these ideas about myself frightens me a little because:

_____

Each day that I no longer carry these outdated ideas of self, I will feel:

_____

I imagine that this newfound sense of emotional freedom feels:

_____

I feel more authentically myself when I:

_____

Take a breath and sit with your responses. When you are ready, think about the insights you now have about the toxic people in your life. What have you discovered about these relationships? Remember, this exercise is not about making changes in your relationships because of your new understanding. It is about looking within, evaluating yourself and your life, and asking yourself what you want your life to look and feel like.

You are doing such good deep work. For years you have wanted to look at these issues, and now you are finally doing it. Take your time. Don't rush. This work is for you and no one else.

Remember to be gentle with yourself today.

HURT PEOPLE FIND HURT PEOPLE

People often attract people into their lives who "mirror" them, or have wounding that is complementary to theirs. We tend to attract and be attracted to someone who carries the wounded emotional signature that we understand. For example, someone who carries the wounding of a victim will subconsciously attract someone who carries the wounding of an abuser. We don't do this consciously, but this is the meaning of hurt people finding other hurt people. This is how our codependent wounds play out in our relationships.

Your Wounded Mirror

In this chapter you will explore your own attraction of and to people who mirror your wounding. These exercises can be quite enlightening, as you will start to identify more clearly the people who you have in your life as a result of your inner child wounding.

EXERCISE: YOUR WOUNDED MIRROR

To determine your wounded signature and who you attract because they mirror your wounding, complete the following sentences:

Even though they are bad for me, I like this type of person:

_____

because when I am around them, I feel:

_____

I have been told that I change when I am with this type of person:

_____

Even though I know what to do and how to be with them, I know that they are:

_____

I am attracted to toxic or chaotic people because they remind me of:

_____

When I am with someone who is energetic and bigger than life, I feel:

_____

When I am with someone who is reserved and quiet, I feel:

_____

I want to be with this type of person:

_____

because he or she represents:

_____

I look for these qualities in someone I want to date:

_____

When I don't find someone with these qualities, I usually settle for:

_____

All my friends tell me that I need to stop:

_____

I feel I can be myself when I am with this type of person:

_____

I realize that these two people in my life are just like each other:

_____

I have the same types of dramas play out with these two people:

_____

When I try to set a boundary with these two people, all I get back is:

_____

Setting a boundary with a person who mirrors a wounding back to me is hard because:

_____

It is easier to stay with them or keep them as a friend because:

_____

I have discovered these patterns and trends about myself:

_____

To transform and heal these patterns, I need to do this:

_____

To help me integrate what I have just learned about myself and my relationships, I need to do this:

_____

_____

When I have set boundaries in the past, the other person talks me out of them. I let this happen because:

_____

When I try to set boundaries with one person in particular, they get really angry, and I feel:

_____

If I got in touch with my feelings, I would feel:

_____

Wounded Partnerships

Couples often replay their wounding scenes with each other, but what happens if you are healing your wounded, lost inner child and your partner's wounding is still raging? Unfortunately, this pairing is more common than you might think. Remember, we unconsciously attract people who have something we want to learn and explore about ourselves, so the wounded self attracts someone whose wounding interweaves and corresponds with its own.

Your partner may not have the same type of wounding that you have, but it mirrors your wounding. They have emotional responses that you understand. You know how to adapt to them, and they to you.

I think I married my mother.

The expression, "I married my mother (or father)" is this sort of scenario. We know how to interact and respond to this unique personality combination. We don't consciously set out to find a mate that has characteristics like one of our parents, but we all can think of someone who keeps dating or marrying the "wrong" type of person.

It is very common for an individual to unconsciously attract a partner who carries the same wounding profile and dynamics of the parent with whom the person had the most disagreements. This phenomenon is not tied to gender, and it doesn't make logical sense, but it is one way that the wounded child tries to heal and move on from a dysfunctional dynamic. Subconsciously we believe that if we are with someone like that parent, then this part of us will grow and heal, and we can move on from the painful roller coaster. In many cases, tension enters the relationship when one partner is healing and growing, learning to find their voice, and setting boundaries, and the other partner wants to continue the dysfunctional dance.

In any relationship, even loving and functional ones, people find themselves at a different stage of emotional maturity than their partner. This is normal, and couples often learn how to successfully navigate these emotional benchmarks. When one person is moving ahead and the other continues to play out the old dramas, this can create a recipe for disaster, but it can also provide a catalyst for growth and expansion of the relationship.

You do not need to leave your partner just because you are in two different places. If you are healing and growing and your partner wants to stay put, then you need to learn how to communicate more effectively. For any relationship to be healthy, there must be good communication. You must be able to express your feelings and what is happening inside of you. You must learn how to express what is going on with you so that your partner is fully informed about where you are emotionally and what your needs are.

When I am working with someone who is learning more about themselves, I often ask how their partner or family members feel about their healing work. Common answers are either, "They don't know I'm coming to see you," or, "They know I'm here and are OK with it, but they don't feel they need any therapy." In other words, a partner or family members may be supportive, but they don't want to know details, or don't think they have any issues that need to be addressed. The person who is in therapy may then feel isolated and invalidated. They are working to understand themselves but are in relationship with someone who turns a blind eye to the uncomfortable realities within the relationship.

I DON'T WANT TO TALK ABOUT IT

Sometimes when people begin to do this work, they realize how much they avoid communication with their partner because their partner doesn't want to get involved. They know their partner's hot buttons, and they make an effort to avoid upsetting them. Withholding like this is very damaging over time because the expression of true feelings becomes scarce in the relationship.

A red flag in my practice is when couples say they never have any arguments. This tells me that one or both of them are withholding some truths that need to come out for the relationship to be functional. They are monitoring and adapting themselves to the other to avoid conflict. This way they can convince themselves they have a good relationship because they don't argue. However, this way of thinking is not logical; it is based on their own emotional wounding.

Usually the inner child wounding is acting out the withholding behavior. The lost inner child is showing up in the adult relationship and shutting down or using avoidant behaviors learned in childhood as a way to cope with an uncomfortable situation. Often, one or both partners will make a value judgment on the feelings they have about an issue and think, *I know if I bring this up, my partner will say this, and then we will get into it again.* As a result, they see communication as futile. By avoiding, they keep this simmering pot of hurt feelings on the back burner. Unfortunately, it doesn't take much for the pot to suddenly heat up and the feelings to boil over.

Avoidance in the relationship reinforces a wounding from an earlier time, and the couple ends up extending the period of emotional wounding expression. They delay the inevitable conversation, which, when it finally happens, usually devolves into an argument, and they express hurtful things. But emotions don't have to come out in this destructive way.

If this is how your wounding is showing up in your relationship, look back over the boundary statements under Wounded Partnerships. How can you express your deep feelings in a loving way? Here are some examples of how to start these difficult conversations:

- I have something I want to tell you, and it is hard for me to say.
- I love you, and there is something I want you to know that I have been thinking about.
- I need to let you know something that has been on my mind. Is this a good time?

Using language like this prepares the listener to know that you have something important to talk about and that you are being thoughtful in how you are approaching them. For most couples, this is a totally different way of speaking to each other, and it is going to sound weird at first. But like any new skill, it will feel more comfortable after doing it a few times. Think of it this way: however you are speaking with your partner isn't working anyway, so what do you have to lose in trying this new approach?

Grieving the Loss of the Familiar

As your therapy progresses, you will probably begin to see, for the first time, blatantly unhealthy behaviors in the relationship dynamic, including sarcastic or demeaning comments from your partner, or outright abuse. As you heal your lost inner child, you are connecting with your feelings, and the reality of your relationship is going to be revealed. This reality may be in stark contrast to how your lost inner child has deceived itself into thinking that the relationship is what it wants it to be.

This realization is very difficult for most people. I have sat with countless people throughout my career who were stunned at the emotional reality of their relationship. Of course, this reality has been there the whole time; they just healed enough to see it. Once they woke up to the reality and took it in, they began a period of grieving for the loss. They realized that the hopes and dreams they had for the relationship would never happen.

This experience was famously outlined by the work of psychiatrist Dr. Elisabeth Kübler-Ross in her book *On Death and Dying*,[1] in which she wrote of her theory of the five stages of grief and loss.

According to Kübler-Ross, the five stages of grief and loss are:

- denial (*I can't believe this is happening.*)
- anger (*I am so angry that this is happening.*)
- bargaining (*If I were to do this, it would make that better.*)
- depression (*I am so sad that this is happening.*)
- acceptance (*I am beginning to understand that this really did occur, and I am learning to accept this new reality.*)

People in grief can bounce around through these stages until they work through the complicated feelings related to a loss. When my parents passed away, I sometimes experienced three or more of these stages all in the same day, and multiple times throughout the day. For me, the stages were like the five points of a star. I would bounce around from one to the next, sometimes throughout the course of a single day.

(If you are going through a loss, whether it is a loss in your relationship or the loss of a loved one, know you are not alone and help is out there. Don't try to toughen yourself up to get through it. There are specially trained people who can create a safe place to you to rest, renew, and recover during this time of painful transition.)

---

1 *On Death and Dying: What the Dying Have to Teach Doctors, Nurses, Clergy and Their Own Families*, Elisabeth Kübler-Ross, MD, Simon & Schuster, New York, NY, 1969.

Going through periods of grief and loss in the life cycle of a partnership—especially a long-term partnership—is natural. If you are understanding more about yourself and recognizing that the relationship is no longer working for you as it stands, now is the time to connect with your feelings and find your voice.

If you find yourself in such a situation, you can open communication by learning to express boundaries to your partner.

GRIEVING AND BOUNDARY STATEMENTS

Mark the boundary statements you would like to be able to say:

- I am confused about why you don't share with me what you are doing and interested in anymore.
- I feel irritated that you are on your phone even when we are sitting next to each other.
- I feel lonely and isolated when you don't notice me or ask me how I'm doing.
- I love you and am committed to you, but I miss our intimacy.
- I feel hurt when you make sarcastic comments to me about things I am interested in and enjoy.
- I feel angry when I have asked over and over for your help with the kids but you do not help me out.
- I feel frustrated when we talk and you say that we will work on our issues, but then you never make the time to do so.

Do any of these boundary statements capture the sense of loss that you feel? Mark the ones you would like to practice on your own, and say them out loud when you are alone to get used to speaking your truth. Your losses need to be honored and expressed so you can move on from them.

You cannot make any decisions about your next steps until you know how you feel about the situation from an emotionally grounded place. If you feel high emotions or your feelings are clouded, this is not the time to be making big life decisions. Give yourself the gift of time, healing, and perspective before you go into your next adventure. You have been on this journey for a while now, so you don't need to rush to any conclusions.

RELATIONSHIP
TRANSFORMATIONS

As you do the work on yourself and heal your lost inner child, your primary relationship, your family, your friends, and your coworkers may begin to notice that something is different about you but can't put their finger on what it is. You look the same and act the same, but something has changed. What is happening is that you are healing from the inside out.

Essentially, when you do this work, you are renovating from the inside, and sometimes the outside appearance changes, too. I often wish that I could take a "before" picture of someone who is beginning the therapy process and "after" picture at the end of their work. Their faces open up, and they have softer eyes and contented smiles. They have a deep calm sense about them after working hard to connect to their authentic selves.

This transformation happens on a deep, subconscious, energetic level. Shifts are occurring within you that are very subtle, and you may not be consciously aware that this is happening. However, others will see, sense, and feel your responsible adult self coming through.

For example, as a person heals an abuse history and begins to have a stronger sense of self through boundary setting, they will no longer carry a victim energy; they will shift their internal reality to that of victor. This creates a totally different relationship with themselves and changes how they relate to others. Carrying this victim-to-victor idea forward, we can imagine that by setting stronger internal and external boundaries, this person will say *no* a lot more. They will be less likely to roll over and do what someone else wants, or at a minimum they will think to themselves that they don't want to do something. They may even begin to walk differently or carry themselves in a more confident manner. As others watch this person unfold, they notice something going on but can't identify exactly what is expanding. If you are going through something like this, you may hear people ask if you are OK, or say that something has changed about you, they just don't know what.

Recall my story and my challenges with my dad in my early life. By the time I began my therapy work in my twenties, I had pushed my anger down, but I didn't see myself that way. My internal view of myself was that I was open and connected, but I wasn't either of those things, I just wanted to think that I was. I couldn't acknowledge my anger, and I didn't want others around me to see how I was actually feeling. As I went through my process, I did a lot of work on my own with my therapist, but not with my dad. Over time, as I developed more self-love and respect, and more love and respect for my dad, my relationship with him softened, and we became more connected. I became more grounded and not as sarcastic or passive-aggressive.

Sarcasm is the language of anger.
It has a smidgen of truth and the punch of biting resentment.

The relationship transformation between my dad and me happened within me, from the inside out. I wasn't looking for him to fix me and make our relationship better. I had to make this better for myself first, then our relationship could improve and expand. Thankfully, that is what happened over time.

My sense is that my dad could essentially feel my shift. I no longer carried anger and resentment toward him. I felt love and respect for myself first, and I wasn't blaming him for anything. I was able to see his totality, his pain, his fears, and his courage. I believe that when we do this work within ourselves, we energetically shift our emotional relationship with others.

I didn't talk with my dad about my own therapy work until much later in life. By then, though, our relationship had healed to such a degree that I didn't need to say anything; we just felt and knew it was better and healed. Because I learned to love and respect myself and in turn was able to love and respect him, I healed and embraced all of those parts of myself that were like him and that I had resented.

Transforming Your Relationships

People who love and respect you will notice and appreciate your work at the level they can meet you. Give others in your life more credit than you had in the past. Know that as you grow and expand, they may be able to grow with you. Hold this intention and hope for your relationships. It is not always a given, but don't limit your beliefs of others; let your intention for yourself expand to them.

Not everyone is ready to transform, and some people in your life may not respond in kind to your transformation. Remember that just because you are changing, it doesn't mean that others will.

Practice standing up and speaking your truth.

EXERCISE: TRANSFORMING YOUR RELATIONSHIPS

I would like to transform this or these relationships in my life:

_____

To heal this relationship, I need to work on this:

_____

To transform this relationship, I have done these things so far:

_____

I am tempted to give up trying to heal this relationship because:

_____

I am carrying these resentments toward the other person:

_____

This is how I feel about the situation:

_____

I want to feel better about this relationship because:

_____

I am trying to be good to myself by doing these things:

_____

Self-affirmation: I am worth loving, honoring, and respecting my feelings and working through my inner child wounding.

CREATING DEEPER, SAFER CONNECTIONS

Transformation is a slow and gentle process. You don't need to do a dramatic overhaul of your life to get it done and out of the way. Doing things in that way is similar to a crisis response behavior, which you may have learned in your childhood family. The HEAL process you have been learning is a gentle unfolding of yourself with yourself. You are recognizing how your wounding shows up in your relationships. You are seeing how you may have responded in the past by getting big and loud or by making yourself smaller and invisible.

Your Safe Connections

Notice where you have safe connections, where the connection feels reciprocal, grounded, and nurturing. Now look at those areas where the connection feels uneven and you don't walk away feeling good about yourself or the connection. This is about observing your interactions with yourself and others and where you are using the tools you have learned. This isn't about judgment; it is about using your discernment to determine your role as a creator or a reactor. Notice where you are doing a good job at staying grounded and where there are some gaps in your functional response tools.

EXERCISE: MAKING DEEPER CONNECTIONS

This exercise builds on the work you did in the Circle of Connection exercise. You will explore your resistance to making deeper connections, which will help you to eventually soften and open to the relationships you want to have.

Complete the following statements to help you see why you don't let your inner circle of people in closer:

I would like to feel closer and more heartfelt to those inside my circle, but:

_____

Opening up my heart is difficult because:

_____

I want to be more heartfelt and open with safe people, but:

_____

When I try to go deeper within myself and open up, I start to feel:

_____

When I do open myself up to those who are safe for me, I often feel:

_____

I see others being vulnerable with me, but I can't go deeper with them because:

_____

Within my circle of safe friends, when I have tried to go deeper with this person:

_____

they won't open up to me.

My safe friends know a lot about me, but they don't know this:

_____

I don't want to share private information with my safe friends because:

_____

The one safe friend who I would like to be closer to is:

_____

I hold back on developing a deeper relationship with this safe friend because:

_____

I have noticed that when I open up to friends they will often:

_____

When friends don't respond to my opening up, I feel:

_____

To take my friendships to a deeper level, I need to:

_____

I don't want more friends; I just want a close circle of friends who are:

_____

Safe people outside my circle who I would like to know better are:

_____

I can tell that this person: _____
who is outside my circle wants more, but I feel:

_____

No one can make you feel inferior without your consent. —Eleanor Roosevelt

CREATING A MORE POSITIVE OUTLOOK

You are reconnecting with your authentic self, the calm and wise place that has always been inside of you. It was covered up by the illusions that others projected onto you and by your own misperceptions of situations. You are learning how to encourage positive self-talk and promote the authentic self to come forward and thrive.

Negative Self-Talk

Words are very powerful, especially those words we use to bring ourselves down or lift ourselves up. Most of us don't realize how many times a day we unconsciously correct or criticize ourselves. Negative self-talk feeds on itself.

EXERCISE: A MORE POSITIVE OUTLOOK

See if you can calm your negative inner voice down and be the change you want to see in the world by starting with yourself. This exercise will begin to help you bring a more positive outlook into your inner world. First you will recognize and write down the negative thoughts you tell yourself. Then you will begin to create more positive thoughts.
Complete the following sentences:

These are all of the negative thoughts I regularly tell myself:

_____

_____

I don't think I can stop my negative thoughts because:

_____

I tell myself negative thoughts because these things happen to reinforce them:

_____

_____

Letting go of the negative thought that I am:

_____

is difficult because:

_____

I am going to try to suspend my negative thoughts. To do this, I need to:

_____

I know my negative thoughts aren't helping me, but if I let them go, then:

_____

The one person who would be shocked that I have these negative thoughts is:

_____

I know others in my life don't see me as a bad person, but:

_____

Today I want to have positive self-talk as others see me, but:

_____

I think I can neutralize these negative thoughts:

_____

In order to move on, I give myself permission to forgive myself for:

_____

Today I will say these three positive things about myself:

　　1)

　　2)

　　3)

When I think good things about myself, I feel:

_____

Others pick up on the fact that I feel better about myself because they see me:

_____

I think I can keep saying positive things to myself if I:

_____

I want to make a commitment to myself to be more positive because:

_____

If you find it hard to say anything positive about yourself, see if you can just neutralize the negative thoughts for now. An example of this is: *I used to say I was stupid and an idiot. Now I say to myself that I am trying my best, but I am not perfect. I want to say that I am a good person, but I am not quite there yet.*

Expanding and Contracting

As you heal yourself, you may no longer fit into your outdated paradigms. You are expanding, not contracting, and you can no longer shrink yourself to fit into old ways of thinking and feeling. Much like a sweater you have outgrown, you do not fit into relationships that no longer serve you. You can make yourself smaller to fit into someone else's world, but comfortably staying there is going to be hard.

As you heal, you are expanding in your consciousness, perspective, and awareness. You now see and know much more than before, and you can't un-see this. You are also feeling more feelings; that is a natural outcome of this process. Perhaps you haven't had these feelings in a long time. You are preparing for a new way of interacting with yourself and others, and are uncovering feelings you have covered up.

EXERCISE: FEELING CONTRACTED AND FEELING EXPANDED

In previous exercises you thought and wrote a lot about your relationships. Think back about what you wrote, then complete the following sentences:

I feel small and contracted, and I don't want to speak my truth or feel my power, when I am with:

_____

I make myself smaller with this person because if I don't, they will:

_____

When I become larger and more myself, they react by:

_____

I need to stay small with this person because:

_____

I learned how to make myself small and invisible because:

_____

When I get small, the people around me remind me of:

_____

I don't want to be small around this person, but if I am not, I am (feeling word):_____
that:

_____

I keep these people in my life because:

_____

FEELING EXPANDED

I feel larger and expanded, and can speak my truth and be authentic, when I am with:

_____

I feel expanded with this person because they feel this way about me:

_____

When this person sees me being myself, I feel:

_____

I know that I can be myself with this person because they are:

_____

Other people with whom I can expand and be myself include:

_____

_____

I feel I can be my authentic self when I am in this sort of situation:

_____

I value the connections I have with authentic people because I feel:

_____

Notice what you felt or observed as you filled in the blanks. What insights do you have about the people in your circle?

_____

_____

STORYTELLING: FACT OR FICTION

When people feel nervous or insecure and want to feel more in control, they often make up stories in their minds about what others think or feel about them, or fill in the blanks about what is happening in a situation. This process is referred to as storytelling, mind reading, or fortune telling. This projection of fear or insecurity comes from an unhealed place. By telling themselves stories, people are trying to make themselves feel safer, stronger, and in control.

Storytelling usually develops in childhood, when a child's needs are not met or the child is hurt, confused, or violated in some way. A trigger develops from this core wounding, and the lost inner child begins to make up stories that align with this original wounding and their own fears. As the years go by, the inner child continues to spin the same elaborate stories when it is triggered. But rather than make things better, these magical stories make things worse. The storyteller begins to believe their worst fears about themselves, someone else, or a situation. The root of storytelling is found in insecurities and anxieties, not trusting oneself or someone else, and carrying fear or worry.

I don't think she likes me. Why hasn't he returned my text? I bet she thinks I'm stupid. I think he doesn't like me. I bet I have that illness I read about. What if this happens and everything goes wrong? These are examples of stories that people make up to fill in the blanks. Most of these stories contain a lot of fiction and little fact. They take a little information and extrapolate a story that matches their fears and insecurities.

Making Up Stories

People often know that they make up stories, but it is hard for them to stop because the stories satisfy the mind, which wants to complete the story. Our minds like to have things neat and tidy, and making up stories is a way to reassure the mind that it knows what is going on. Anxiety also plays a major role in creating what-if scenarios. *What if I don't get my job promotion? What if this illness is really serious? What if I don't get to go on my vacation?* If you are a storyteller like this, then building trust in yourself and others is important to heal this part and to stop the internal wounded narrative.

Suppose you send a text to a good friend, and they don't respond in the time they normally do. You start to make up a story as to why they haven't responded. You wonder what is going on, and if they are OK. After a while, you start to worry about your friend. If you are insecure, you begin to make up stories. *Is she mad at me? What did I do? Maybe it's because I didn't say I wanted to go with her. Maybe it's because she doesn't really like me. I know! It's because the other day I said I didn't like what she was wearing.*

People also tell themselves stories about a situation they are worried about. Suppose you notice that you are having problems with digestion. Then you remember that a friend was recently talking about someone who had a really bad illness that had started with their stomach hurting. At this point, you may start a story about your own problem, and if you are prone to worry, your story will grow into a full-blown fear that you have the illness your friend was talking about. You start filling in the blanks as needed so that your made-up story matches how this illness looks and feels. Now you start to believe the story. You research the illness on the internet, and notice that the symptoms are getting worse. Now fearful, you make an appointment with your doctor, who tells you you're fine. You just ate something that gave you gas. Of course, we need to listen to our bodies and honor the signals we receive, but you can see how the what-ifs can quickly get out of hand.

I have heard many people make up super-scary stories about themselves or a situation. They worked themselves up and got agitated because they had convinced themselves that the fiction they had created in their minds was true. This type of storytelling is called catastrophizing or exaggerating, and we have all done it at some point in our lives. You can see how storytelling can get the better of us and can ruin a perfectly pleasant day.

To stop storytelling, you need to take some simple steps within your mind, but they are difficult to do in the moment because making up stories is so much easier.

Recall the example of your friend not returning your text. Here is another outcome: If you notice the text hasn't been returned in the time your friend normally returns a text, make a mental note of it. After some time has passed, notice whether you are starting to make up stories or not. If you are, then ask yourself whether the story is fact or fiction. Tell yourself, *All I know is that I texted her. She will get back to me when she can.* If the storytelling persists and fears bubble up, take some deep breaths and think, *I know that the last time we talked, we had a nice conversation and everything was OK between us. She will get back to me when she has time. I trust her.* What you are doing is reassuring yourself with a set of known facts. You are going back to your last interaction with her, reminding yourself of the quality and depth of your friendship and connection. You are calming yourself down and reminding yourself of what you know to be true so that you don't start to make up fictional stories out of worry.

I know this sounds easy, but it is hard to do. For the most part, people today are impatient, and want answers and responses quickly. This impatience comes together with insecurities, worries, and control and trust issues, creating a perfect storm for storytelling.

EXERCISE: ARE YOU A STORYTELLER?

We often tell ourselves stories because we want to feel in control. In this exercise, you will determine when and about whom you make up stories. Complete the following sentences:

The most common story I tell myself about myself is that I am:

_____

The person who I do the most storytelling about is:

_____

I make up the most stories about this person because:

_____

I make up stories because I feel this way about the relationship:

_____

I know that I make up these stories, but I can't stop it because:

_____

When I make up stories, I feel that I am:

_____

If I stop telling myself these stories, I would feel:

_____

I want to feel in control and know what is going on with others. This is related to my feeling this way as a child:

_____

I tell myself what-if stories all the time, especially about:

_____

I probably started making up stories like this as a child when this happened:

_____

I know my inner child needs to hear this from me to help calm down my storytelling:

_____

I tend to make up stories in these types of situations:

_____

_____

Basing my thoughts on facts alone is hard because I want to make up stories. This is because:

_____

When I want to calm myself down and trust that things will work out, this is what I will tell myself instead of making up a story:

_____

_____

SHAME

Feeling shame when we do something wrong is a natural part of emotional life. Shame serves many purposes in society and in life in general, and we experience it throughout our lives. When shame occurs in childhood and is not put into context, the lost inner child can carry the shameful feelings into adulthood. Shame comes from behavior that the child or adolescent did themselves or that was done to them. Often the child merges their identity or self-worth with the shameful thing they did or that was done to them. When this occurs, the shame becomes toxic. This is the origin of the "shame monster."

Healthy shame helps to reset ourselves when we veer off the path of doing what we know is right. When we observe and honor shame, we can examine our feelings, forgive ourselves, and move on. Being overwhelmed by shame, and being unable to forgive oneself to get past it, can develop into toxic shame. Toxic shame is when people cling to their shame and have feelings of worthlessness. Discerning the authentic self can become very difficult because the toxic shame is so loud inside.

Shame and guilt are two different emotions. Shame is a feeling we have *about ourselves*, as in, *I am a mistake*, and guilt is a feeling *about a situation*, as in *I made a mistake*. Healthy shame is when we feel ashamed that we have done something we know is wrong according to a set of social standards. We feel badly about our choice, and most of us try to make amends at this point. Unhealthy or toxic shame is when we believe that our poor choice says something about *who we are as a person*. We personalize the experience and take it in deeply, rather than just seeing the choice as an error.

The Shadow of Shame Monster

Sometimes after someone has revealed a shameful secret, they feel overexposed and remorseful. I have had strong, intelligent men and women who were so nervous to tell me something they were ashamed of that they almost fainted in my office. The reality is that it wasn't me who they were concerned about, it was themselves. They didn't want to admit out loud whatever it was they did or what they thought about, because they were ashamed of it. They didn't want to look at it or hear themselves say it, and they didn't want to reveal it to someone else.

That said, one of the great advantages of working with a therapist is that a nonjudgmental person listens to you. When someone else truly hears your emotional truth, deep healing occurs, and you begin to lay part of that burden down. As you talk about what you are not proud of and bring this truth out of the shadows, you begin to develop a relationship to that part of your history. No longer is shame hidden in the shadows, jolting you out of bed at two in the morning. Working on your issues with the HEAL process will give you many of the same exercises an inner child therapist or attachment trauma therapist would ask you to do.

As you do this work, give yourself the gift of forgiveness for the choices you have made that didn't work out well. Chances are you set out with good intentions, but something happened, and things changed. That is a normal part of life. Sharing your story with someone close to you can be very powerful and take you to a deeper level of healing within yourself and a deeper connection with your friend. It is not the same as going to see a therapist, but when someone else is a witness to your story, healing occurs.

Be careful who you share your shame feelings with. Try to discern whether they can emotionally hold space for your vulnerability.

> *Once we expose shame to the light of day,*
> *the power we had been giving it fades away.*

Transgressions we have done toward another or that have been done to us are not easy to heal or even let go of. If this is the case for you, you many need to make amends to yourself or someone else for these choices. The reality is that we all make mistakes, that each of us is perfectly imperfect.

EXERCISE: THE SHADOW OF SHAME EXPOSED

The following exercise will help your wounded parts find the courage to go into the Shadow of Shame and look at those things that cause you distress. Be gentle with yourself during this exercise. Know that you don't have to mark up this workbook with your responses if you are not ready to look a particular shameful thought or deed just yet.

Do this exercise in a quiet space if possible. Remember, be gentle with yourself.

Complete the following sentences:

There is something that I am ashamed of that I have held on to for a long time, probably_____ years.

I wish I could just let go of the memory of this shame. I have tried to do the following so I don't have to think about it:

_____

Whenever this shame comes up in my mind, I immediately feel:

_____

I have gone back over this event so many times wishing I had made another choice, but all this does is cause me to feel:

_____

I feel very alone with this shame, and if others knew what I had done or how I feel about it now, they would:

_____

My shame involves someone else, who told me to keep it a secret, and because of this I feel:

_____

I want to tell other people in my life about this shame, but I am afraid that if I told them, they would:

_____

I sometimes think I am the only one who has done something like this:

_____

What I need to tell myself about what I am ashamed of is:

_____

Each day, in every way, I can begin to hold and honor this part that I am ashamed of by doing:

_____

I know that today I would not make the same choice. I trust that, for whatever reason, what I did seemed like the best choice at the time. Here is why this is hard (or easy) for me to accept:

_____

I have shared my shame secret before, and it didn't go well because I now realize:

_____

I am going to try to forgive myself in small ways each day for what I have thought or done in the past. I can do this by:

_____

_____

If I can't let go of this shame on my own, I will make a commitment to see a therapist so that I no longer have to carry this burden. Write your commitment here:

_____

_____

I know that going into the Shadow of Shame is not an easy assignment. However, with practice you will find that the more you acknowledge and interact with those things you are ashamed of, the less power they have over you. What was it like for you to look at those things you are ashamed of? Come back and do this exercise as often as you are moved to.

SPEAKING YOUR TRUTH

Many people don't speak their truth because they think that if they do, others may not be able to handle it. They decide for someone else whether that person can handle the truth or not, instead of trusting the other person to think for themselves and decide what they want to do with what they hear. Other reasons that people don't speak their truth are that they don't feel strong enough, don't feel they have the right to, or have been ignored in the past when they did speak their truth. There are many reasons why people stifle their feelings, but they only hurt themselves in the end.

Using "I" Statements

Using "I" statements communicates a feeling you have in reaction to what someone has said or done. These statements are not about blaming or shaming others, they are used to express a feeling you have and to identify a behavior by the other person. When you express yourself in a way that fosters open communication with the other person, you communicate your feelings and honor yourself instead of creating closed-off defensiveness.

Here is an example that blames the other person and talks about their behavior instead of naming a feeling you have: "I feel you are manipulating me! Stop manipulating me!" These statements do not encourage an open dialogue. They are expressions of blaming, frustration, and anger. Statements such as these create a defensively guarded wall of words, and the other person will most likely become defensive upon hearing them.

Using the same theme, here is an example of claiming and naming feelings and clearly identifying the behavior of the other person: "I feel hurt and disrespected because at times you say mean things to me. Also, it seems that you are trying to convince me I am wrong when you correct my language." This can be followed by stating what you need: "Going forward, I need [this behavior] from you."

See the difference? The first example sets you up for a yelling match or a defensive conversation. The second example expresses your feeling and then names the behavior the other person does that you are referring to, followed by a statement of what you need from them.

As a side note, we often hear the common expression, "They made me feel this way." This statement blames another person for how we feel, which puts us in the place of being the victim. The reality is that other people cannot make us feel a certain way. What we feel is an emotional response to an outside stimulus. We are responsible for our own feelings, what we do with those feelings, and how we express them.

EXERCISE: USING "I" STATEMENTS TO EXPRESS YOUR TRUTH

This exercise will help you to connect with a truth you would like to speak but have been reluctant to do so. Using the chart in table 3 as a reference for feeling words, you will practice writing "I" statements to express how you feel about something. Do your best to choose exactly the right feeling words for each statement. (Notice that "OK" and "I'm fine" are not listed. Consult the Feelings Chart in table 1 in the introduction if you need more feeling words.)

TABLE 3. FEELING WORDS, SHORT LIST

afraid	aggressive	angry	anguished	bewildered
curious	cautious	blah	blissful	blue
bored	calm	confident	confused	crushed
delighted	determined	despondent	disapproving	disappointed
distressed	ecstatic	enraged	envious	exasperated
exhausted	fearful	frightened	frustrated	grief-stricken
grouchy	happy	hurt	idiotic	indifferent
insecure	joyful	pained	perplexed	proud
regretful	relaxed	sad	satisfied	secure
shy	suspicious	threatened	tranquil	undecided

Here is the "I" statement format: I feel (emotion) when you (behavior), and I would like (behavioral request).

Following your "I" statement by expressing what you need going forward is important. This last step clearly gives the other person the full context of feelings and what they can do to help you in the future.

For example: "I feel *hurt* when you *say bad things about me*, and I would like *that to stop*. I need to hear what I am doing right, not just what I am doing wrong or how I am wrong.

Here is another example: I feel *really happy* when you *take out the trash*, and I want *to thank you for that. I need to know going forward that you can do this without my asking.*

Complete the following statements to see with whom or where you need to speak your truth.
I need to use an "I feel" statement with this person:

_____

I have been reluctant to say anything to that person because:

_____

If I were to speak my truth, it would sound like this:

_____

I don't think my truth would get a good response because:

_____

I have tried to speak my truth before, but this always happens:

_____

I don't want to speak my truth anymore because:

_____

If I spoke my truth, then this would happen:

_____

Continuing to suppress my truth is OK because:

_____

I can keep denying my truth because doing so is easier, and I am:

_____

If I could find the courage and strength to speak my truth, this is what I would say:

_____

When I write out what I want to say, I feel:

_____

I know I may not be ready to speak my truth right now, but I can prepare to speak my truth if I do this:

_____

I look up to these people because they speak their truth:

_____

I am going to work on my fears, insecurities, and lack of self-trust myself by:

_____

To work on these issues, I will need to:

_____

I can find the courage and strength to do so because I have done this courageous action in the past:

_____

Self-affirmation:
I am a work in progress,
and each day I am getting stronger,
owning my power,
feeling my worth,
speaking my truth,
and loving and respecting myself more.

SYMBOLIC LETTER WRITING

When you have lingering frustrations, resentments, or irritations, a good way to transform this energy is to write symbolic letters. Much like the healing letters you wrote in Part I and the Mad Lib style writing you did earlier in Part II, symbolic letters are just for you, and they are not meant as a record or diary. The time to write a symbolic letter is when you just can't move past an issue, when it keeps coming up and nagging you and you just want it to go away.

However you choose to ceremoniously clear the energy between you and another person is up to you. The action of writing out your feelings will bring clarity of feeling and mind, and give you a sense of acknowledgment and validation. Nothing may change between you and the other person that you can consciously determine, but subconsciously you are working behind the scenes and cleaning house of those heavy emotions that clog your filter and no longer serve you.

Symbolic Letters

Symbolic letters are not meant to be given to anyone else; you are just doing this internal work and handling your part of it. If you feel the need to talk with the other person about an issue, symbolic letter writing will help you clarify exactly what you feel. As a precaution, remember to manage your expectations before speaking to the other person. Remember that they probably haven't been working on being as intentional with their emotions as you have, and they may not be coming from such a grounded place.

EXERCISE: SYMBOLIC LETTER WRITING

Do this exercise when you can devote about fifteen minutes or so.

Center yourself in your emotions so you can have clarity with your intention. Focus your mind on what has been irritating you. Do not preplan what you want to write. On a clean sheet of paper or new e-file, start writing your letter to the person toward whom you are irritated, frustrated, or have resentments.

Write fast and furious, and let it all come out. Keep writing until you no longer have anything to say. You are cleaning house and getting it all out of you.

When you no longer have anything to say, stop and reread what you wrote. Then rip it up or delete it. You may even want to shred or burn this symbolic letter as a way to get closure.

Once you have written this symbolic letter, complete the following sentences to see other areas this exercise will benefit you:

I need to write a symbolic letter to these people:

_____

I would like to write a letter, but if I were to, I would feel:

_____

I don't think this would do any good because:

_____

I would be tempted to give the other person the letter, but:

_____

I have tried talking to this person in the past, and I:

_____

I keep thinking that I want to write a symbolic letter, but I stop myself because:

_____

I am scared to write a symbolic letter because I feel:

_____

To help me integrate the new energy I feel after writing a symbolic letter, I can do these things:

_____

_____

As you do this healing work, you will find that symbolic letter writing is a great way to clean house and get out of you all that energy that is stuck and no longer serves a purpose. It is also a great way to clean out your filter and get you back in the flow of life.

FILTERING

You have learned a lot about how your lost inner child controls and affects many of your reactions to triggers. Another way to look at this is that all of your interactions are passed through a filter. Everyone, everything, and every situation you have ever encountered from childhood on has been run through this filter. The filter has developed from your self-perception, your emotional wounding, your healing, and all of your life experiences. All of the unhealed emotional wounding of the lost inner child is captured in the filter.

Your Personal Filter

Your filter is unique to you, and you view yourself and the world through it. If your filter is relatively open and clear, then you see yourself and others realistically and authentically, and you have good judgment of life in general. However, if your filter is clogged and cluttered with many unresolved emotional wounds, then everything you run through it will be interpreted through a cloud of uncertainty and fear. When your filter is clogged with heavy, distracting boulders of unresolved situations, getting through life takes a lot energy. This clogged filter inhibits you from setting good boundaries, holding you back from developing healthy, functional, and happy relationships.

Each clog in your filter affects your sense of self. For example, if you have an ongoing control struggle with someone, you may have made up stories as to why you are right and they are wrong. You give a lot of energy to this big boulder of a control struggle inside of you. As Saint Augustine wrote, "Resentment is like drinking poison and waiting for the other person to die." This sounds harsh, but if you think about all of the unresolved issues you are holding on to, you may realize how much energy you spend each day to maintain that dirty, clogged filter. You have to try to look through a cloudy filter of issues to see the good in yourself, in your life, and in other people, and that is a lot of work.

How do you know whether you have a dirty filter or not? Ask yourself if you have a pessimistic, negative outlook a lot of the time. Do you have anxieties, fears, and worries? Are you sad, depressed, and see only bad things happening? These are all indicators that your personal filter is clogged and that your inner child is lost.

The more you have inside of your filter, the more clogged and distorted your perception of the world is, which also affects your thoughts and feelings about yourself and drains your energy.

EXERCISE: WHAT IS CLOGGING YOUR FILTER?

This exercise will help you to determine what is in your filter so that you can clear it out. You can come back to this exercise at any time as you heal to continue to clear out your filter.

The illustration in figure 3 represents your filter. Inside the filter, write down the issues that you think are clogging it. For example, you have a disagreement with someone that has lasted for years and is still not resolved, or some childhood issues from your timeline that bother you, or something happened in your adult life that still weighs heavy on your heart.

On the outside of the filter, write down issues you have healed. For example, you worked through an issue with someone else and reached a resolution, or you moved on from a toxic relationship that no longer served you.

Are there a lot of clogs inside your filter? If so, have most of these emotional boulders been there since childhood? Or have they mostly developed in your adult life? Do you see a pattern?

_____

_____

What issues are clogging your perception of reality that you think you can begin to heal?

_____

What changes do you need to make to create this healing?

_____

If there are many issues that are clogging your filter, use the parts of the HEAL process you have learned to address these emotional wounds. You now have the tools to use at any time to work through the issues that come up in your life.

Now look at the items you wrote down outside of the filter. Notice how you have cleaned up issues that at one time had taken a lot of mental and emotional energy. Congratulate yourself on working through them. Remember that you are the creator of your reality, and you can change and control your self-perception.

FIGURE 4. YOUR FILTER

FEELING STRONGER EVERY DAY

Each day, and in every way, you are getting stronger as you begin to know yourself in a deeper, more connected way. You have learned how to acknowledge your wounding and use your new functional tools, creating a plan to heal yourself going forward.

As you heal, your wounded parts are putting down the wounded emotional response tools and impulsive reactions, and learning to trust your responsible adult self to be there. Your wounded parts know and feel that your responsible adult self is setting functional boundaries. These parts don't feel as guarded as before and are loosening up. Your wounded parts are no longer stranded and frozen in time. You are joining and integrating these parts with your responsible adult self.

A New Part of You

Now that your wounded inner child is feeling stronger and not as wounded, you may wonder if you can call this part of you something other than "lost" or "wounded." The answer is YES! There is another way to refer to that part of yourself. You have done some incredibly hard work, and you can develop a new name to call the part of yourself that is healing.

EXERCISE: RENAME THE HEALING PART

You can rename the healing part of you whatever you want. This exercise will help you find just the right words. Some people call this healing part "younger me" or "little me." How you name it is up to you, but it is important to recognize what that part sounds and feels like and for you to know when it shows up.

If you need ideas for how to refer to your healing inner child, think of a nickname you would give a young person in your life whom you love. You can also use the following list to find a word or phrase that accurately describes this part right now, today. The idea is that you will reference this part as your "fun size" coming out and wanting to connect.

Here are some nicknames for the inner child: champion, hero, friend, buddy, macaroni, bug, fun size, sweet self, glow, bright spot, spark, child self, love, tender spot, pal, bestie, little part, nugget.

Consider the following questions, and then write down the characteristics of your healing younger self:

Does this younger part still become triggered in the same way, or is it softening and not as reactive?

Does it still feel as young as it did at the beginning of your work, or does it feel a little older and a little wiser?

Is your responsible adult self stepping up for your inner child and setting boundaries consistently, or is this haphazard?

Complete the following sentences to describe what your healing inner child sounds, feels, and acts like. Use the most specific terms you can.

The inner child part of me feels this way now:

My inner child no longer feels:

My inner child has learned:

My inner child feels whole when I am with these people:

My inner child feels whole when I am in this type of situation:

_____

My inner child still feels this way with these people:

_____

_____

My inner child is scared to let go of its wounded tools because:

_____

My inner child keeps showing up and impulsively reacting because:

_____

The responsible adult part of me needs to do this so my inner child feels safer:

_____

My inner child is still wary of the responsible adult self because:

_____

Going forward, this is what I will tell my inner child each day:

_____

Going forward, this is what I will do for my inner child each day:

_____

For my inner child to fully integrate with my responsible adult self, I need to:

_____

Letting Go of Attachment to an Outcome

Expectation is when the mind thinks something is going to happen—expecting a certain outcome and wanting control—rather than being in a state of wonder or hope for an outcome, akin to anticipation. When you expect that a certain thing will happen or that a person will react a certain way, you are attaching an expectation to the outcome.

Expectations usually happen quietly inside, and we don't even realize we have them. For example, you are excited about giving someone a birthday gift, and you subconsciously expect that they will respond a certain way. Or you are looking forward to a vacation or job assignment and have specific expectations.

The list of expectations you have each day would probably amaze you. They range from the small and mundane—*I'm going to make this green light*—to the profound and eventful: *I expect to get this job.* Expectations are completely natural to have. The problem arises when we have unrealistic expectations or when we wish that something specific will happen or that a person will change.

People will ask if they are not supposed to have any expectations, and I don't think that is possible or realistic. We all put expectations on ourselves and others; it is human nature. Our minds like certainty, and the mind will start to craft an expected outcome or a guarantee very early in the process. The mind does not like surprises, and it likes to be in control. The important part to remember is that expectations are not guarantees of outcome.

I recently heard a story that illustrates this concept well. Chaz had bought his wife a gift for the house that he thought she would love. However, when she opened it, she was not as thrilled as he thought she would be, and he was disappointed. His wife wasn't too happy, either. Chaz had the best intention to please his wife with the gift, but he missed the mark. In his mind, he had set an expectation and attached an outcome to the gift giving the moment he purchased the item.

What are you to do? How do you stop being hurt by unmet expectations? You can change expectation to hope. You do this by setting an internal boundary about how attached you will allow yourself to get to an outcome, and then stay hopeful. If you hope someone likes a gift, there is some expectation, but it is not as intense. If you often feel disappointed, you are expecting too much from a person or situation.

You give yourself a gift by staying in a state of hopefulness. You don't set yourself up for a disappointment like you do when you have expectations. The distinction is subtle, but the emotional weight between expectation and hopefulness feels different.

Abby's story is an example of the disappointment of having an expectation instead of setting an intention. Abby was planning a party for her children and her new stepdaughter to tie-dye some shirts on a hot summer's day. She had gotten all the supplies she needed, and started imagining how her stepdaughter was going to interact with her children. She imagined a happy blended family outcome, the fun shirts, and everything going perfectly. She was unknowingly creating the perfect opportunity for disappointment.

The party went fine and the kids had fun, but the shirts didn't turn out well. Instead of the colors being bright and fun, they were all muddy. The shirts not turning out perfectly wasn't the Hallmark movie moment Abby was looking for. She came away from this experience as if she had failed in some way, and felt disappointed.

When we talked about the experience later, she asked what she could have done differently so that she wouldn't have felt so disappointed. I suggested that she could have not put the pressure of perfectionism on herself, and that she could have transformed her expectation of the outcome into an intentional thought. For example, she could have thought, *My intention is that we all have a fun day. However the shirts turn out is how they turn out. The goal is for us to just spend some time together doing a fun activity.* In this case, she would have hoped that things went well, but she would have given herself permission to let go of a particular outcome.

For someone with trust issues like Abby, hoping something happens is a stretch. Observe this pattern of expectation within yourself, and see if you can move from attaching yourself to a specific outcome to being open for new possibilities and opportunities.

EXERCISE: OBSERVING YOUR EXPECTATIONS

This exercise will help you see when you set expectations and when you are simply hopeful. Consider the events of the last week. Where, what, how, and why did you set expectations? Where were you simply hopeful? Complete the following sentences to find out:

This last week I set a strong expectation and was attached to an outcome about:

_____

I have greater expectations from this person or this type of situation:

_____

I often feel disappointed with this person or situation:

_____

I realize that I set expectations instead of hoping for an outcome with this person:

_____

I have tried to not have any expectations with this person:

_____

I realize that my inner child's unrealistic expectations are connected to this in my childhood:

_____

When expectations are not met, my inner child feels this way:

_____

My inner child expects others to:

_____

My inner child has given up having any expectations for this person or situation:

_____

My inner child feels burned out from expecting:

_____

When I let go of expectations about a person or situation, I usually feel:

_____

I want to feel in control, so I don't like uncertainty when:

_____

I attach an expectation to an outcome because:

_____

Being hopeful instead of expecting an outcome is hard for me because:

_____

If I don't have expectations, people will not know what I want because:

_____

I try to be clear about what I expect from a project, but people disappoint me because:

_____

I need to start expressing myself in this way so others know what I am thinking:

_____

I need to stop assuming people know what I mean when I say this:

_____

I will practice being hopeful about a person or situation by saying this:

_____

SELF-NURTURING

You have done so much hard work as you have examined your feelings and worked through some difficult topics. You need to take care of yourself and your inner child as you move, shift, and expand parts of yourself and create a new reality.

Healing is not an easy journey, and you probably don't consciously realize how much brain power, emotional energy, and physical shifts have been needed to transform your emotional landscape. This transformation cannot be measured or seen, but as you do the work, you are probably recognizing some different feelings that you have never known before or have felt only briefly at times. This new feeling is your lost inner child rejoining with your authentic self. It is you reconnecting and coming home to your own safe place within, where you know this is who you truly are. What a wonderful feeling it is to feel whole and complete.

Elements of Self-Care

To keep this feeling, sustain this energetic transformation, and maintain all of the functional skills you are developing, you will need to continue to create elements of self-care and self-nurturing. Examples of this self-care are doing the things you know you need to do but may not like doing, such as eating well and in moderation, exercising in some form, being with others and not isolating, and maintaining your wellness. The other part of this hygiene involves being conscious of where your thoughts are going and the messages you give to yourself, as your mind will want to go back into those familiar but unhealthy and nonfunctional grooves in your brain.

The most important part to take away from this exercise is knowing that you are in charge of your mind, your mind is not in charge of you, and that you have done a lot of healing work. So even though your mind wants to fall into that familiar wounded groove, you can gently guide and direct it out by simply saying to yourself, *I don't have to go there right now. I am choosing to be positive, and I trust that all is going to work out in my life. I work hard on my healing every day.*

This message pushes trust buttons for some people, and they can't say this to themselves or they don't think it is true. I respect that, and I don't mean to make all of this sound easy and that everyone can do this. If it were that easy, everyone would be doing this work already. The reality is, though, that you *can* direct your thoughts to a different narrative. You do not have to keep telling yourself the same story over and over and running yourself into the ground.

EXERCISE: PRACTICE NURTURING NARRATIVES

This exercise will help you practice saying and believing narratives that nurture yourself as you heal. Read the following messages of self-care and self-nurturing. See which ones you can give to yourself today and which ones you will work on bringing into your consciousness.

Read the following statements out loud. Pause after each one:

- I am perfectly imperfect.
- Each day I am doing the best I can. I know that each day I am putting my best foot forward.
- Whatever I did in my past that I regret, I know that it wasn't my intention to make that mistake. I forgive myself for this.
- I am already good as I am. I don't need to be better than I am.
- Today I am focusing on *being* instead of doing things to give me a sense of self worth.
- I am choosing where my thoughts go and what I focus on instead of turning control over to my mind.
- I am choosing what I want to do with my feelings instead of turning over all of my control to them.
- Each day, in every way, I am living the best life I know how.
- I am learning how to be gentle and loving with myself.
- I am no longer pushing myself with negative reinforcements to be "better."
- I am choosing emotionally healthy people to surround myself with who love, honor, and respect me.
- I know that even though the future is uncertain, I am confident in myself.
- I am taking life one moment and one day at a time.
- I am turning my expectations into hopeful intentions and letting go of attachment to outcomes.
- I trust that I will make the best choice I can in any given moment if I am consciously aware of my choices.
- Even though I haven't ever been perfect or made good choices, I know that I am a good person.
- I know that I am deserving of love.

- I know that I am deserving of respect.
- I know that I am deserving of trust.

After reading this list and centering yourself, how would you describe yourself to someone else?

_____

What aspects of yourself do you want to emphasize and have someone else really hear?

_____

How will you honor those parts of yourself that you are still in the process of healing?

_____

The stories you tell yourself and others reinforce and carry forward your narrative. You can shape your story by recognizing where you have come from, what you have healed, and what you are looking forward to manifesting in your life. As my friend the late Rev. Don Burt once said, "Be kind to the shadow of your former self." Know that you are healing your shadow and that you are shining your light as brightly as you can each time you heal the wounded part of yourself.

As you continue your healing work, talk about where you are today and where you want to go. You have worked hard to heal big parts of your past. Celebrate your uniqueness and who you are today because there will never be another you. Every day, in every way and in each moment, you are the best _you_ that ever was and ever will be.

> **_You can't really love someone else unless you really love yourself first._**
> **_—Fred Rogers_**

ABOUT THE AUTHOR

ROBERT JACKMAN is a board certified Psychotherapist with the National Board of Certified Counselors who has helped many people on their healing path for more than twenty years. In addition to his private practice, he has taught master's level classes at National Louis University in the Chicago area, led outpatient groups in hospitals, given lectures on mindfulness, hypnotherapy, codependency, and the role of spirituality in healing, and participated in numerous weekend retreats with Victories for Men.

Robert is also a Reiki master who uses energy psychology in his practice and considers himself a codependent in recovery, always working on boundary setting, discernment and connecting with his authentic self. He lives in the far west suburbs of Chicago and in Oregon with his family. He enjoys photography, kayaking, gardening, and nurturing and delighting his inner child.

For more information about Robert Jackman, his other works, upcoming events and the *Healing Your Lost Inner Child* book and companion workbook, please visit www.theartofpracticalwisdom.com.

Made in the USA
Las Vegas, NV
06 September 2022